THE ART OF
WRAPPING GIFTS

By
DRUCELLA LOWRIE

GRAMERCY PUBLISHING COMPANY

·

NEW YORK

CONTENTS

The line illustrations in this book are by Helen Disbrow.

The Well Wrapped Gift

Everyone likes to receive a gift, and the way it is wrapped and presented is almost as important as the choice of the gift itself. An attractive package expresses not only the good taste of the person giving it, but also his thoughtfulness toward the friend being honored. It provides something beautiful and tantalizing to enliven the occasion.

On the other hand, a sloppily wrapped package, or one too gaudy or too skimpy, indicates poor taste, indifference, or lack of skill—and inevitably detracts from the pleasure intended. This does not imply that much has to be spent on materials. Even if you use the simplest papers, the package should be neat, without untidy wrinkles or bulges, the ribbon of suitable width and color for the paper chosen, and the trimming artistically arranged on the package.

Learning to wrap gifts is like learning to drive a car; you must do it! There are some rules to guide you, but, like driving, real skill comes with practice. As you try your hand not only will you develop the finger dexterity required, but you will also develop wrapping and trimming ideas that are completely your own. Of one thing I am sure—you will have the greatest fun wrapping gifts; and there will be the satisfaction that in each case you have produced a little work of art of your own.

Equipment and Materials Needed

Most of the items you will need for gift wrapping are small and inexpensive. They should be on hand and kept in one place (a suit box or an old suitcase) so that they are readily available. When you know that you have the necessary materials, you have the incentive for doing something effective and interesting for special occasions. Everyone is conscious of the need for Christmas wrappings, but it is the occasional gift —birthdays, graduations, anniversaries, weddings, babies—which finds many of us unprepared. To avoid last-minute searches for gay papers, fresh tissues, and attractive and suitable ribbons, keep a supply of a few well-chosen gift-wrapping materials in readiness. Any basic supply should include plain tissues in assorted soft colors; a few rolls of plain or colored cellophane; a few rolls of gold, and silver, and other gay metallic papers; and a varied assortment of printed designs.

Make it a habit to walk through the gift-wrapping and ribbon departments when you shop. Beautiful designs and types and colors of both papers and ribbons are constantly being developed and you can buy a little now and then when there is a wide selection to choose from and no crowds to delay your shopping. Also, there is less drain on the budget than buying all at one time.

Figs. 1 and 2. In addition to the tissue and fancy papers, the following supplies will be needed: boxes of varying sizes and shapes (save the good ones that come from stores), scissors, ruler, pencil, seals, Scotch tape, paste, name tags, an assortment of ribbons, tying wire, coarse thread, and a variety of decorative items such as flowers, bells, evergreens, small tree ornaments, and tiny gadgets and knickknacks to suit your personal taste and requirements. With these at hand any of the wrappings demonstrated in this book can be done easily.

One further tip: Throughout the year, cut out of your favorite magazines the illustrations you like best. Many wrapping suggestions given include the addition of a pasted-on illustration: a painting, flowers (for garden gifts), places of travel, a fashion plate, an antique, etc. You can keep these in a manila folder, ready to go through whenever you need one. (See illustration, on page 4, right.)

CONTAINERS

Any gift looks better in a *box;* the box protects it, keeps it fresh and attractive. It is much easier to wrap a boxed gift. Ask for boxes when buying gifts; and save all clean, strong, attractive boxes. Nest them to save space. Buy them if necessary. Jewelry is much more appealing when displayed in a box made especially for it, padded with velvet or satin. Many boxes can be used more than once if kept clean and fresh looking.

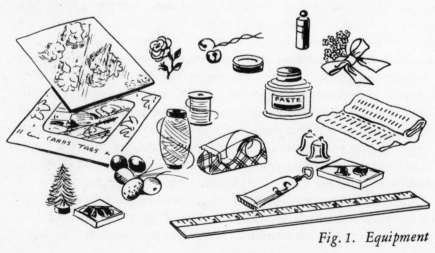

Fig. 1. Equipment

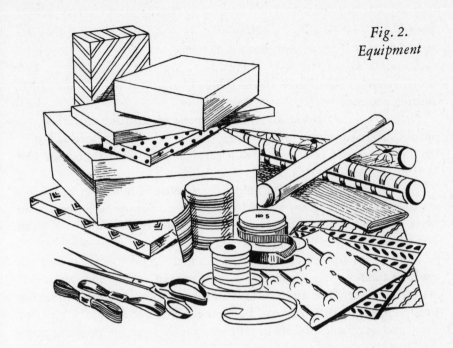

Fig. 2.
Equipment

Boxes come in all shapes and sizes. Choose a box of the right size for the gift. If the box is too small, the contents will bulge and the wrapping may burst. If the box is too large, the contents may slide around inside and break or become wrinkled.

Choose a box strong enough for the contents; heavy or bulky items require a sturdy container. Reinforce inside corners with Scotch tape or gummed paper tape, if necessary.

If boxes are marked with price tags or figures, remove or erase them. *Cover printed trademarks with large seals or with pasted cutouts.* If the box has bold print designs or stripes in bright colors, use metallic or heavy foil paper for wrapping so that nothing will show through to mar the outer effect.

Some breakable gifts come factory packed in corrugated boxes. These boxes can be quickly transformed into attractive gift containers by applying a coat of wallpaper paste and papering with wallpaper or gift paper.

Use tin or plastic boxes for gifts of food and candy. If cardboard boxes must be used, line them carefully with waxed paper, aluminum foil, or cellophane.

Clear cellophane or plastic is used on the lids of many boxes to display the contents. Other boxes are made entirely of "see through" material. Such containers are quite fragile and will require careful rein-

7

forcing with cardboard or a strong outer box to protect them if they are to be handled much or sent through the mail.

Wooden boxes, if not too flimsily put together, will stand up well under frequent handling and will stand the rigors of mailing with little outside protection.

Other types of containers may be made by utilizing materials you would ordinarily throw away. For example, all types of cereal boxes, crackers and cake boxes, ice cream cartons, milk cartons, and the like will make useful containers.

You can make an excellent holder for a bottle of toilet water, a man's pipe, tools, or toys from a quart milk carton. Simply rinse the carton well, cut the top along three sides so that it will open as a lid and wrap the whole carton with gift paper.

Cigar boxes and wooden cheese boxes make good containers and can even be used as gifts if they are given a coat of shellac and, when dry, painted with bright enamel. Coffee and shortening tins are worth saving and painting so that they can be used for gift goods. Many types of fruit and vegetable baskets usually thrown away at the corner grocery can also be salvaged as containers.

Save as many containers as you have room for with the idea of using them later for making a pretty package. When you have a good collection, take a few hours' time and decorate them all. Paint them or paper them; use decals, nail polish, gold or silver paint, poster colors (from an artists material store) for finishing touches. You will be well repaid.

PAPERS

For many years plain tissue paper was the only kind available for wrapping gifts. Then a demand for a stronger paper resulted in the manufacture of a wrapping somewhat heavier than tissue. This was made in a few colors. Later it was printed with appropriate Christmas designs. As the demand for pretty papers increased, the variety in designs also increased, until today we have papers in all patterns and colors, including gold and silver, for every gift occasion.

Textured papers have also been developed. One type looks and feels like suede. Another has a quilted-like surface. Some have embossed designs with raised patterns. Another type of paper is made with glossy enameled finish resembling patent leather, while still another has a dull finish.

Decorative papers come in a wide variety of types and colors, designs and qualities. There are rolls and packages. If you use a lot of paper, there is less waste when you cut just what you need from a roll; but, for the single gift or small box or two, the package containing folded sheets is more economical.

Papers fall into the following categories:

Tissue is a thin, soft paper, plain, ribbed, or creped. Two layers of tissue may be necessary for strength and better color. It may be used under the regular gift paper to keep any printing on the package from showing through. Tissue printed in fine stripes or delicate floral designs is available. This is especially effective for use as an inside lining for boxes holding dainty lingerie, blouses, and baby things.

Cellophane is a clear, tough plastic-type wrapping. It is widely used to cover flowers, food, toys, or any item whose beauty or interest is to be seen, yet protected. Cellophane comes in many colors. A good grade may be twisted or crumpled without tearing.

Solid-color papers are made in both dull and glossy finish and are always in good taste and suitable for any occasion. They vary in price depending on the weight and texture. Suede and embossed-finished papers usually cost a little more than regular sheets. All solid-color papers make a fine background for printed ribbons.

Metallic papers are made by coating a regular paper with a film of metallic paint. Other types are made by laminating a layer of metal foil onto a paper backing. They come in a wide range of beautiful colors. Those with printed designs or embossed surfaces may again cost a little more than the plain paper. Aluminum foil, which is not a paper but a thin layer of aluminum, is used in place of paper to wrap food, bottles, and many other forms which have odd shapes. The foil can be pressed to conform to the shape of the container.

Printed papers are made by a process much like that used in making wall paper. The design is etched on metal rolls which pass through troughs of color, and the imprint of the design is left on the paper as it passes swiftly between the rolls. Other, more unusual designs are printed by a hand screen process which is slower and therefore more expensive. The skill of the artist, the method of printing, the type of color used, and the quality of the paper are all factors which enter into the price you must pay.

You can find a print suitable for almost every possible occasion: birthday, wedding, shower, graduation, holidays. There are special children's designs with bright-colored toys and animals. Bold plaids, geometric patterns and stripes, wood grain, sporting motifs are available and are particularly good for the masculine gift.

Other types of paper suitable for gift wrapping are: *Wallpaper,* which is sometimes used for wrapping gifts, is quite crisp and unyielding and tears easily. *Crepe paper* is elastic and tough and is fine for decorating baskets and odd-shaped items. *Shelf paper* with its pretty borders may be used for a kitchen gift. *Square paper doilies* are good for small packages.

TYING MATERIALS

Ribbon is the most universal decorative tying material. The ease with which it may be manipulated, its general availability, and the wide price range make it ideal for this purpose.

Ribbon is woven on looms into various widths and has a woven selvage which keeps it from fraying. It has been used as decoration for centuries.

Cut-edge ribbon is a more recent type. Acetate rayon fabric is cut into ribbon widths with a hot knife which melts the fibers and fuses the edges to form an *artificial* selvage.

Ribbons are made in an endless variety of types, colors, widths, and textures. The most familiar types are listed below.

Satin ribbon, the most popular ribbon for packages, is smooth and glossy on the right side, and plain and duller on the reverse side. When the satin finish is on both sides, it is called double-faced satin ribbon. If two colors are used, one on each side, it is called two-toned, double-faced satin.

Grosgrain ribbon has crosswise ribs. It has a firm body and may be used for tailored bows, as well as for tying gift packages. *Faille ribbon* has finer ribs than grosgrain and is not so firm.

Taffeta ribbon is closely woven and has a crisp finish. It has no right or wrong side and is widely used for crisp bows.

Moire ribbon is a taffeta ribbon with a wavy watermark. It is most effective when used on plain paper.

Picot edge ribbon is a ribbon with tiny loops in the selvage which gives a decorative appearance.

Changeable taffeta is made by using two different colors in the weave, one for lengthwise and one for crosswise threads.

Velvet ribbon has a pile that varies in softness and thickness with the quality of the ribbon. Its rich appearance makes it ideal for tying expensive gifts such as jewelry, silverware, heirlooms.

Novelty ribbon identifies many fancy combinations of weaves, colors, and finishes. Stripes, checks, plaids, flower prints, and polka dots are the most popular. It is used for special-occasion gifts.

Metallic ribbon is woven of silver or gold strands. These are sometimes combined with rayon or silk fibers to make a beautiful and flexible ribbon.

Novelty tinsel ribbon combines sheer fibers with strands of gold or silver in a gauzy-type or firm-type weave.

Gauze and ninon ribbons are woven with fine threads for a sheer effect and may be either crisp or soft. They are used extensively on baskets, flower arrangements, and packages.

Plastic ribbon, cut in rather wide strips, may be glossy or dull and is waterproof. It is particularly suitable for decorations which are exposed to the weather.

A *threadlike plastic* fiber is shaped into *lacelike* designs and pressed into bands of assorted widths. It looks as delicate as fine lace, yet is crisp and washable. Its trade name is Lacelon.

Another ribbon is made of satin and has an adhesive on the wrong side so that it may be pressed on like any tape. Its trade name is Sattex.

Laminated ribbon, a new type of gift tie with an exceptionally brilliant sheen, has been developed in the last few years. It has a glossy, silk-like appearance and is made by laminating long rayon fibers to an acetate film. It is known by various trade names: Satin-glo, Texray, Facile, Glamortie.

A ribbon made from long cotton fibers glued together and rolled flat, then crimped lightly, is known as ribbonette or crinkle-tie. It is very strong.

Ribbonzene is made from rayon fibers glued together and crimped. It is one of the original low-priced gift-tying materials.

Numerous combinations of fibers combined with cellophane, tinsel, and rayon appear each year as cords or ribbons under various trade names.

Printed ribbon for gift tying is very popular. Designs are available for every purpose—baby, birthday, showers, Christmas, and so on. It personalizes the package and emphasizes a specific occasion.

Fluorescent ribbon. Gift-tying satin ribbon is now dyed in fluorescent colors which have a dramatic, glowing sheen.

A table of standard ribbon widths is given here* for convenience in ordering a specific ribbon width by number. Manufacturers designate ribbon widths as No. 1 (about 1/4 inch), the narrowest, to No. 120 (4 1/2 inches), and for fashion purposes up to 16 inches.

---

* See top of page 12.

No. 1 ▬ about ¼″

No. 1½ ▬ about ⁵⁄₁₆″

No. 2 ▬ about ½″

No. 3 ▬ about ⅝″

No. 5 ▬ about ⅞″

No. 9 ▬ about 1½″

No. 16 ▬ about 2¼″

No. 40 ▬ about 3″

MISCELLANEOUS MATERIALS FOR GIFT WRAPPING

The package with a professionally wrapped look is much more tempting and exciting to open than one haphazardly tied together. To achieve the professional look, the following items will prove helpful:

Scotch tape comes in transparent or colored rolls and is practically indispensable for securing box lids; sealing package ends; attaching bands, bows, or trims. Colored bands of Scotch tape may also be used to decorate packages. Dispensers designed for holding the roll of Scotch tape make for speed and efficiency in handling.

Seals, plain or matching the design of the paper, can be used to secure and hold the corners and places where the paper overlaps. Thus there need be no loose edges to tear and spoil an otherwise attractive package. Some people use rubber cement, paste, or gummed tape to make the package firm.

Pins (small straight ones) are sometimes used for pinning bows or bands to the box.

Gift cards and tags. There should be cards to enclose in the package, as well as tags, for identification on the outside. Parcel post labels should be on hand.*

Decorative trims, such as bells, ornaments, flowers, can be as extensive and as varied as your imagination will allow. Suggestions for attractive package decoration will be found throughout the book.

Wire. Pliable spool wire, the kind used by milliners and florists, is much used for bow making and attaching decorative trims to packages.

Wrapping paper for mailing should be strong yet pliable enough for easy folding.*

---

* See page 88 for additional notes about packing for mailing.

Color Combinations in Ribbon and Paper

The selection of the right color for a gift wrapping is very important, for it is perhaps color more than anything else that makes a package distinctive. The old stand-bys in color of ribbon and paper are always good, but there are so many interesting and unusual color combinations that the individual who experiments with colors will get increased pleasure from wrapping the gift.

Some of the more *unusual color combinations* are chartreuse and cerise, purple and silver, moss green and bronze, lime and blue, mauve and purple, deep red and forest green, royal blue and kelly green, pink and purple, brown and mustard yellow, and so on into the bright colors used together in painted folk art designs like pink and dark green on bright red, bright blue, yellow and red, etc. For the latter bright and gay effects it is almost a necessity to work with three colors in paper, ribbon and trim, you will soon get the idea if you study some illustrations of early American folk art or Mexican and European painted boxes and furniture.

When plain papers are used, choice of color in ribbon becomes simply a matter of personal preference; but when a printed paper is used, one of the colors in the design should be matched in ribbon. If you match one of the lighter colors the effect is dainty. Use the dark colors with discretion or the package may look heavy.

If two or more colors of ribbon are used on the package, use more of one than the other. In other words, make a large bow of one color and a small one of another color as an accent. Or use wide ribbon in one color and narrow ribbon in another.

Floral printed ribbon, polka dots, stripes, checks, plaids, and other novelty ribbons may be used freely with plain papers.

Dark papers are rich looking when trimmed with metallic ribbons or any of the brilliant colors in harmonizing tones.

If you are not sure of your taste in color, be guided by color combinations found in expensive wallpaper, drapery and dress fabrics, paintings, flowers, and even in good gift-wrapping paper and greeting cards. Such designs are created by artists whose sense of color can be trusted. Note carefully how the artist balances his colors—sometimes a lot of one color with just a touch of another.

At the top of the next page are some of the standard color combinations which you are always safe in using.

Paper	Ribbon
light gray	any color
white	any color
silver	any color
red or pink	white, green, yellow, blue
yellow	green, white, blue, red, brown
blue	white, pink, yellow, chartreuse
gold	red, pink, green, blue, mauve, yellow

As there are many shades of each of these colors, it must, of course, be up to you to pick the shade of red that goes with the shade of blue, etc. The pastel shades go well together, but there can be no general rule. On gray, white, and silver paper, these colors being neutral, any color you like in a ribbon will be set off attractively, and the same holds true in nearly all cases for gold.

How To Wrap Your Gift

Certain steps should be followed if you would make a beautiful gift package:

Preparing the gift
Boxing the gift
Selecting the paper
Wrapping different kinds of boxes
Selecting the ribbon for the package
Tying the ribbon on the package
Making bows (glamour, loop, pinwheel, poinsettia, hair, wreath, corsage, Greek, pussy cat, figure-8, basket, tied)
How and where to place bows on the package
Adding decorative trimmings

PREPARING THE GIFT

Remove the price tag. If item is wrinkled, press it. If gift needs dusting, polishing, decorating, or trimming, do whatever is required. Fold and pin, if necessary, to make gift look attractive when lid of box is raised.

BOXING THE GIFT

Fig. 3. Most gifts should be boxed. If no box comes with the gift, be sure to select one that is the right size. Line box with tissue paper as

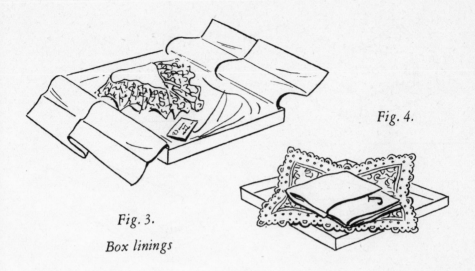

Fig. 4.

Fig. 3.

Box linings

shown. Add gift card bearing your name and fasten lid securely with Scotch tape to prevent bulging.

Fig. 4. A lace-paper doily makes a dainty lining for a handkerchief box. Fold the corners of the doily over to the center, add gift card, then put the lid on and wrap.

SELECTING THE PAPER

The choice of paper is largely an individual matter. However, certain basic rules should be observed for the best results. Use large designs on large boxes, and vivid colors and small designs on smaller packages. Diagonal stripes, vertical lines, geometric figures, scenes, and any of the plain, softer colors are ideal for the large package.

Pick the color and design with the recipient in mind. For boys and men, choose masculine colors, designs, or textures. Women love floral patterns of good design, rich exotic colors, or delicate pastels and all the feminine frills. All sorts of amusing patterns are designed for children and the colors can be as gay as you wish.

Many papers are designed for special occasions such as anniversaries, birthdays, weddings, etc. It is convenient to keep a supply on hand.

When using rolled sheets of paper for wrapping, unroll all sheets, place roller on right side and reroll. This reverses the curl and makes the sheets lie flat. If the folded paper is deeply creased, press out with warm iron before using.

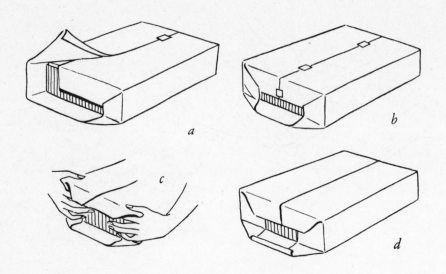

Fig. 5. Making a neat package

WRAPPING DIFFERENT KINDS OF BOXES

In the paragraphs which follow, wrapping directions are given for the small rectangular box, the deep box, large suit or blanket box, hat box, books, cylinders, bowls, jars, wine bottles, and irregular boxes.

The secret of making a neat package lies in the way you handle the paper. Don't bundle the box with a lot of excess at the ends and corners. Cut the paper to proper size. Draw it smoothly around the package and hold it with tape while you fold the ends in as flat and smooth as possible (see *Fig. 5a*). If there is excess bulk, simply cut it off with the shears. A neatly papered box is a "must" if you would have the ribbons or other trimming show off to best advantage.

The small rectangular box (Fig. 5). Tape the lid to the box to prevent bulges and to add firmness to the box. Lay the box upside down on the paper. If the paper has a pattern or printed message, make sure the design is properly centered on the box so that it shows off to best advantage. Allow enough in width to overlap 2 to 4 inches. Paper should extend at ends no more than three-fourths the depth of the box. Lap one edge of paper over the other and fold in top edge ½ to 1 inch to make a firm edge (*a*). Secure with Scotch tape, seals, or paste.

Fold ends as shown in illustration (*b*) or, in the case of a deep box, as in (*c*). Fold narrow hem along edge for added strength (*d*). Secure with seal, tape, or paste.

The deep box *(Fig. 6)*. This may require two sections of paper. Set the box right side up on the wrong side of the paper. Bring sides up as far as paper will come, and hold with tape. Fold ends as in illustration (*a*). Turn box upside down on second sheet of paper and cover lid, sides, and ends. Allow paper edges to overlap about 2 inches. Cut away excess paper, if any, and save for small packages. The edges where paper laps (*b*) should be covered with ribbon.

On many boxes the paper is not quite long enough to meet or lap. In this case cut an extra piece of paper and paste it to the bottom of the box. Then wrap as usual. The ribbon trimming can be arranged to cover the place where the paper was spliced.

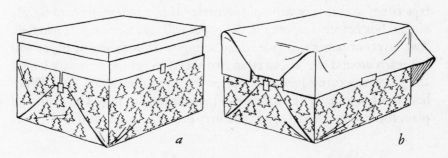

Fig. 6. The deep box

Fig. 7. Some boxes, not deep enough to need two papers, may be covered by wrapping the lid and box separately. To cover the box, cut paper two inches wider than box and long enough to reach around it. Spread

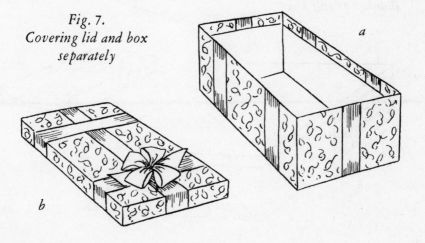

Fig. 7.
Covering lid and box
separately

paste along top and bottom edges of box, then wrap the band of paper completely around the four sides. Clip corners. Fold 1 inch of the paper over the top edge of box and paste to the inside. Fold 1 inch under box at bottom (*a*) and paste lightly to hold edges fast. Cover lid with same or contrasting paper, allowing 1 inch to fold inside lid. Secure with thin layer of paste. Clip at corners and make a neat overlap. When dry, the box and lid can be decorated as shown in (*b*). Combine papers for unusual effects; printed paper on box, plain on lid and vice versa; or plain color on half of box, another plain color on other half, or the same color all over, relying on the ribbon alone to give contrast.

Large suit or blanket box (Fig. 8). First, make box rigid, if necessary, by adding a piece of stiff cardboard to top and bottom or ends, and tape edges so that they will hold securely. If box bulges, tie cord tightly around box before wrapping or the paper will tear when box is handled. Two layers of paper will give added strength. If one sheet of paper will not reach around the box, overlap two sheets to get the necessary length and paste or secure edges with tape as shown in illustration (*a*). Wrap bottom of box first (*b*). Splice two more sheets for top. Use print and plain for novelty effect (*c*), or you may paste the edges of three or four

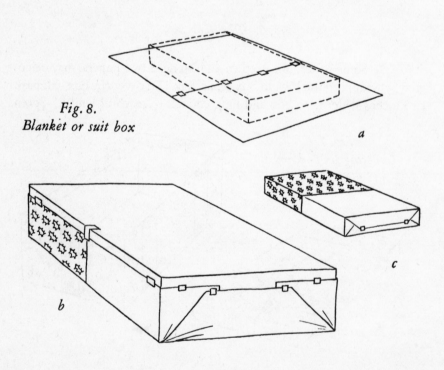

Fig. 8.
Blanket or suit box

a

b

c

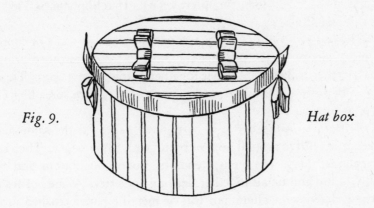

Fig. 9.   Hat box

sheets of paper together to form one large piece and wrap it around the box in the usual manner.

Books. There are many ways of wrapping a book and because it is such a popular gift item it deserves special attention. If it has an attractive title, or jacket, simply wrap it in cellophane to keep it clean. Tie with narrow ribbon, matching one of the colors on the jacket.

Or you may simply cut a book cover from gift paper and fold it over the hard covers as you would a school book. Tie a ribbon around the book lengthwise and make a bow at top edge (see page 51).

You can wrap it to look like a shoulder bag and add a ribbon shoulder strap, or, of course, you may place the book in a box and wrap as you would any type of gift.

Hat box (Fig. 9). Cover sides with a length of paper wide enough to go around the box and deep enough to fold inside at top ½ inch, and to fold under bottom ½ inch. Paste paper on box by applying paste to the box, *not* the paper. Cut a circle of paper slightly larger than the lid. It may be necessary to slash the overlap at intervals to ensure getting the overlap flat on the edge or rim. Brush paste lightly on lid and around edge, lay paper in place on lid, and press edges over the side. Cut a narrow band of paper long enough to encircle edge of lid and paste in place. This narrow band may be of plain paper to make a contrasting trim. Allow to dry and, if necessary, trim edges neatly with a razor blade. Such boxes are strong and especially acceptable as closet accessories.

Cylinder (Fig. 10). Cut paper slightly longer than the cylinder to be covered. Roll paper around cylinder and seal. Fold ends neatly as shown in illustration (*a*). Cover with a large seal. Or leave one end of paper long and tie, then fringe by cutting the paper into narrow strips and add stars, if you like, for interest (*b*). If cellophane is used, the ends can be fluffed (*c*).

Bowls, jars (Fig. 11). Cut squares of cellophane in same or contrasting colors. Set bowl, jar, or other container in the center, then bring all edges together and squeeze paper together at top of container. Tie with ribbon. Be sure you allow enough paper to give a nice spreading effect at top, as shown.

Wine bottle. Wrap bottle in corrugated paper cut the same length as the bottle. Fill in around neck of bottle with tissue paper. Then cover as a cylinder (*Fig. 10*). Paste ends of ribbon on bottom and wind spirally to top and tie all together, leaving ends free. Wine bottles may also be covered with aluminum foil or metallic paper crushed around neck of bottle. Or they may be wrapped in cellophane, which is then twisted at the top.

Irregular boxes. Heart-shaped, triangular, or octagonal boxes are best covered by cutting and pasting top, bottom, and sides to fit. This requires time and patience, but boxes so papered are often kept for a year or two and used as utility boxes around the home. If the original box is beautiful, as are many candy or jewelry boxes, no wrapping is necessary. Protect it from soiling by covering with cellophane, or it may be placed inside a larger box and wrapped in the customary manner.

Fig. 10. Cylinder shapes

Fig. 11. Bowls and jars

As soon as all the packages are wrapped, put away the remaining paper and clear the working surface so that you will have ample room for tying and bow making.

SELECTING THE RIBBON FOR THE PACKAGE

Choose the color that harmonizes or contrasts with the paper, and a width that is in proportion to the size of the box. The wider ribbons are used on large boxes. In place of one strip of wide ribbon you may substitute two or three rows of narrow ribbon; or you may use the wide ribbon across one side with two or three rows of narrow ribbon across the end. Sometimes two or three rows of narrow ribbon are more pleasing than one wide band.

Do not use ribbon so wide that it will cover most of the design on the paper. If the paper has a distinct motif which has been properly centered on the package, use the ribbon across the ends or corner so that it does not cover the pattern on the paper.

Use narrow ribbons on small packages.

Do not combine too many kinds of ribbon or too many colors or widths on one package or it will appear cluttered. Be especially careful to select appropriate colors and widths of ribbon if you are using a printed paper. If in doubt, always keep the effect *simple*.

TYING THE RIBBON ON THE PACKAGE

In applying the ribbon, line and balance should be considered. For example, the ribbon should be applied to conform to the size and shape of the box (centered on a square box; toward the top of a long, thin box, etc.). Ribbons should be smooth, straight, and evenly spaced.

Fig. 12 shows the most common method of tying a ribbon on a package. Lay one end of ribbon on top of the box in the center. Hold with thumb of left hand, leaving 4 or 5 inches of end free. With right hand,

21

Fig. 12.
Tying ribbon on box

wrap ribbon around ends of box, cross at right angles, and wrap around the sides of the box. Bring to center and tie in a hard knot. Cut ribbon, leaving two ends of from 4 to 6 inches for attaching the bow. *The bow should always be made separately and then attached to the package.* Vary the placement of the ribbon by winding it around one end and along one side, or by tying separate pieces around each end of the box. Paste or tape ribbon ends to hold. The ribbon may also be wound around the side of the box. (See opposite for other suggestions.)

Corner (diagonal) wrap (Fig. 13). To tie box in diagonal effect (*a*), hold the ribbon with thumb at center of the top end of box, bring across top left corner, under lower left corner to bottom center. Now bring ribbon up across lower right corner and under upper right to starting point. Tie in a double knot at or near starting point. To make the double diagonal effect (*b*), turn the box and continue as above, crossing the other two corners.

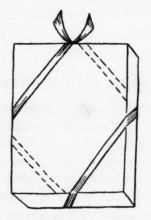

a

Fig. 13.
Corner wrap

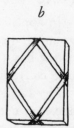

b

22

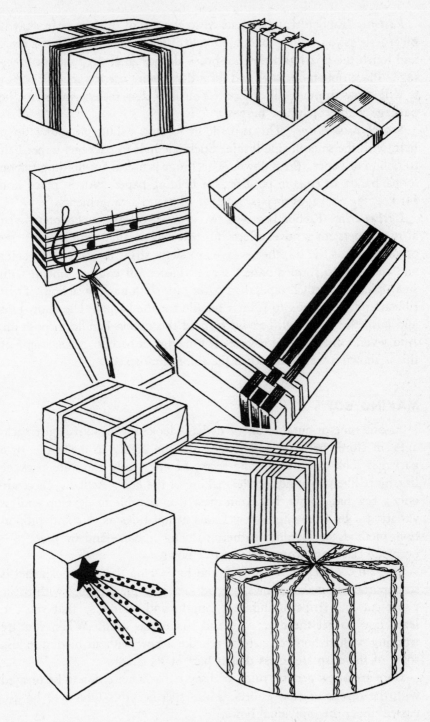

Fig. 14. Different ways of wrapping boxes

Pasting. Ribbon may be attached to the top of the box only. Lay it on exactly as you want it to look, then lift the ribbon, one piece at a time, and touch the box lightly with a brush dipped in sticky paste or mucilage. Place ribbon on paste and let it dry. Don't use too much paste or it will show through the ribbon. You may also fasten ribbon to the package with Scotch tape hinges.

Scotch tape hinge. This is made by folding a short piece of tape in half, with the smooth side inside. Stick one half to package, upper half to ribbon or paper. Press down. This hinge is useful for holding ribbon loops, bands, or ends in position, for holding paper folds in place, and for keeping packages or jars together in group arrangements.

Basket trim. Ribbon bands of two or more colors may be interwoven at the corners for a novel effect. Or you may arrange lengthwise strips on one half of the lid, then weave crosswise strips in contrasting color and cut ends to form a basket shape. Fasten all ends of ribbon with small pieces of Scotch tape, then cover tape with narrow ribbon. Twist ribbon and pin to box to form a handle for the basket. Use short pins and push them through box lid to hold the ribbon handle in position. Add several small ribbon rosettes at top edge of basket. An example of this is shown toward the left in the color frontispiece.

MAKING BOWS

At one time or another all of us have looked at beautiful gift packages, in stores perhaps, and longed for the ability to make our own packages look as perfect. The secret of any really exquisite package lies, more likely than not, in the making of the *bow*. Actually, there are only a few basic bows, but from these it is possible to develop endless variations. By following a few fundamental rules as to color, proportion, methods of looping, gathering, tying ribbon—and by practice—everyone can learn to make attractive bows.

To gain confidence in yourself, and to develop the deft touch that is so important in making bows, a good idea is to practice first with tissue paper cut into strips of different lengths and widths so that you can learn how to get the exact size and shape you want. When you are working with ribbon you cannot remake a bow without having it lose some of the crisp freshness that is part of its charm.

Here are a few general rules to observe if you are going to be pleased with the results of your efforts. More specific procedures will be discussed under the individual bows.

1. Always make the bow separately and then tie it onto the package.

2. Make loops in proper proportion to the width of the ribbon. The narrower the ribbon, the shorter each individual loop should be, and the more loops you need to have a puffy bow.

3. Be lavish with ribbon and make plenty of loops. In general, keep loops the same size. Special effects with long and short loops will be discussed further on.

4. When pinching ribbon together to form loops, make *tiny* pleats or gathers.

5. If you are using ribbon with a right and wrong side, be sure to keep right side out at all times by turning the ribbon as necessary before making a loop.

6. Do not handle the ribbon more than is absolutely necessary.

7. Wind bows *tightly* in the center with fine wire, thread, or narrow ribbon. For fluffy upright loops and with laminated ribbons wire gives best results.

8. Fluff out the loops with your fingers and arrange in a symmetrical and attractive manner.

As you can see, there is no "black magic" or specialized knowledge required—bow making is a skill which lies within the reach of everyone.

The following bows are described: glamour bow with five variations, loop bow with seven variations, pinwheel bow with one variation, poinsettia bow, hair bow, wreath bow, corsage bow, Greek bow, pussy cat bow, figure-8 bow, basket bow, tied bows with two variations.

GLAMOUR BOW. Fig. 15. The one shown requires 2¾ yards of 2-inch-wide ribbon. Three and one-half inches from one end, pinch gathers in ribbon and hold between thumb and fingers of left hand. Seven inches from this point, pinch gathers again and bring up to first gathers to form a loop 3½ inches long as shown in illustration (*a*). If ribbon has a right and wrong side, keep right side out by turning ribbon under thumb and fingers as loops are made. With right hand, continue making loops in the same way (*b*) until you have twelve loops (six up and six down) and an extra end about 3½ inches long. Wind wire or thread around gathers to hold them in place.

When making this bow, adjust the length of the loops according to the width of the ribbon. If the ribbon is 3 inches wide, you will need 2¼ yards to make ten loops. If the ribbon is 1½ inches wide, it will take 2¾ yards to make sixteen loops. If the ribbon is ½ inch wide, you will need 3½ yards to make a bow of twenty-eight loops. In other

Fig. 15.
Glamour bow

words, the narrower the ribbon, the more loops necessary to make an attractive bow.

You may find it easier to make smaller bows and group two or three together to form one large bow.

Variation 1: twin bow. A glamour bow made from ½-inch ribbon can be nested on the center of a larger one made from 2- or 3-inch ribbon. Use contrasting colors or kinds of ribbon.

Variation 2: carriage bow (Fig. 16). Use 3-inch ribbon and make a glamour bow which has only six loops and two ends. Tie in center with narrow ribbon and arrange loops to form a circle. Make a second bow (using same or contrasting color) having only four loops and lay it on the top of the first bow (center on center). Tie both bows together and attach to package. When made in pink, blue, or white, this bow is especially suitable for baby gift boxes, as it may be removed and used on carriage or blanket.

Variation 3: double bow (Fig. 17). Make bow as in variation 2, but use a different kind of ribbon for the smaller, center bow. For instance, you can use tinsel on satin, gold on green, silver center bow on big blue bow, etc. The one illustrated shows a striped bow on a plain-colored larger one.

26

Variation 4: knotted bow (Fig. 18). This is a very pretty variation. Use ribbon 1½ to 2 inches wide and about 2 yards long. Make a mark every 10 inches (see illustration [a]). Tie a soft, loose knot at every other mark (b). Pinch gathers on the mark *between* knots and make loops as for original glamour bow (knot should come at the center of the loop). This is especially attractive in gauzy tinsel ribbon or soft satin. When made from baby ribbon with knots about 5 or 6 inches apart and with twenty to thirty loops in all, you have a beautiful rosette. It looks pretty on bassinets as well as on packages.

Variation 5: narrow ribbon glamour bow. This is made in the same manner as the original glamour bow, but the ribbon selected should be less than 1 inch wide, and loops should be short and numerous (twenty to thirty). In this particular instance, be sure to wind center *tightly* with wire so loops will stand upright. (See frontispiece, front right package.)

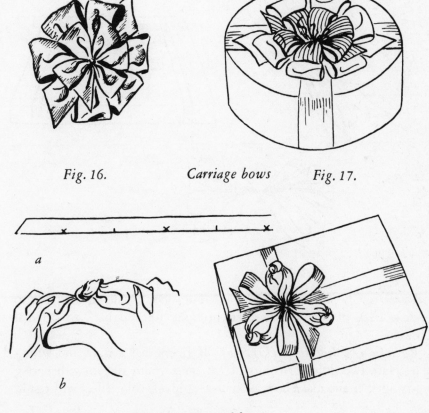

Fig. 16.   Carriage bows   Fig. 17.

a

b

Fig. 18.   Knotted bow

LOOP BOW *(Fig. 19)*. The loop bow resembles a wheel. It requires two yards of ½-inch ribbon—preferably firm or stiff, such as cellophane, laminated, metallic, grosgrain, or ribbonette. Ribbon must be alike on both sides.

Make a 3- or 4-inch loop about 5 or 6 inches from one end as shown in illustration *(a)*. Do not pinch together. Continue looping ribbon back and forth, making each loop directly under the one above, until you have made fourteen to sixteen loops. Wind fine wire around center, taking care not to crush edges *(b)*. Lay on package and spread loops apart at center to form a perfect circle. Fasten to box by pinning through the center, or use Scotch tape hinges.

The circle effect may also be obtained by making two bows of fewer loops each and joining them back to back on the package to form the circle *(c)*.

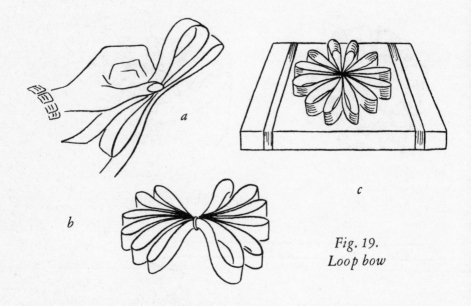

Fig. 19.
Loop bow

*Variation 1: flat edge (Fig. 20).** Turn loop inside out by pushing bottom edge of loop into center, bringing up and back to original position.

Variation 2: two-tone (Fig. 21). If ribbon has a right and wrong side, place two different colors of the same width ribbon with wrong sides together and make bow as shown. A lovely color effect will result.

---

* By permission of the copyright owner.

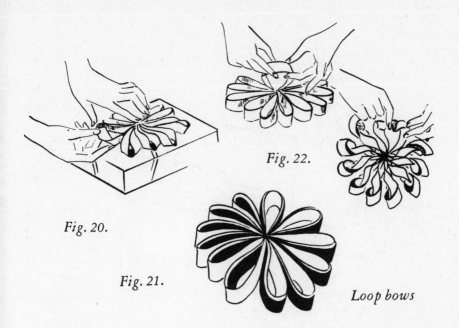

Fig. 22.

Fig. 20.

Fig. 21.

Loop bows

*Variation 3: twisted edge (Fig. 22).** Push loop in toward center. Push top edge down and under so that it turns inside out, to give the twisted effect as shown. Use ribbonette or crinkle-tie.

Variation 4: long and short (Fig. 23). Follow directions given for making the loop bow, but instead of winding the wire around the center, wind it nearer the top so that the upper set of loops will be shorter. This long-and-short version can be used as is, or the shorter loops may be bent down over the longer ones. It is especially pretty when made in two-tone colors as suggested in variation 2.

Variation 5: graduated loops. When making this version, start with a short loop and make each succeeding loop a little longer. You can follow *Fig. 23* as a guide, but do as instructed here, tying in center.

Graduated Loops

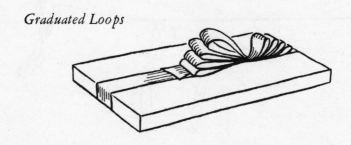

Fig. 24.
Two-in-one bow

a

b

c

Variation 6: two-in-one (Fig. 24). Lay narrow ribbon on top of a different color or kind of ribbon in a wider width (*a*) and form a bow (*b*) in any of the above variations. This will result in an interesting difference between the top and bottom loops (*c*).

Variation 7: layer bow (Fig. 25). For this bow, ribbon must be alike on both sides (moire, grosgrain, metallic, tinsel, double-faced satin). Lay ribbon on a flat surface and fold loops back and forth on top of one another (*a*), making each one shorter than the one beneath. Tie firmly around center and attach to package. One and a quarter yards of ribbon will make a nice bow which has three loops on each side as shown in (*b*).

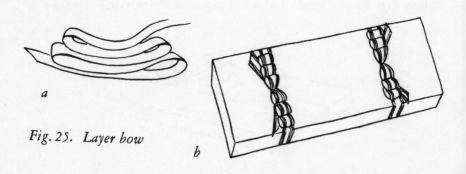

a

Fig. 25. Layer bow

b

If you wish to make this bow of ribbon having a right and wrong side, it may be done by cutting ribbon into graduated lengths and folding as demonstrated on the wreath bow in *Fig. 30.* Fold ends to center and glue or stitch. Lay the longest piece on the bottom and arrange the other pieces in layers. Tie all together at center, then cover the center with a small·piece of ribbon.

PINWHEEL BOW *(Fig. 26).* From 1-inch ribbon cut four pieces, each 5½ inches long. Wind thread around center of each piece and tie tightly. Arrange the four pieces in wheel form and tie together. Cut ends diagonally, in fishtail shape or with pinking shears.

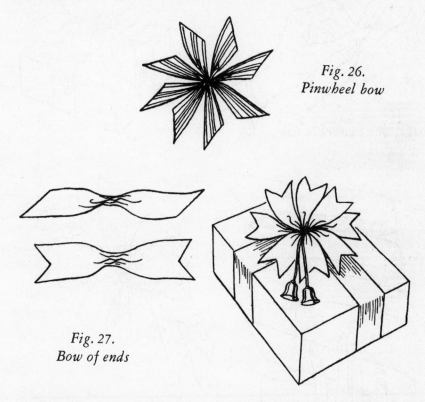

Fig. 26.
Pinwheel bow

Fig. 27.
Bow of ends

Variation 1: bow of ends *(Fig. 27).* Cut ribbon into short lengths. Group five to six pieces (or ten to twelve double length) together, and wind wire around the center. Ends may be fringed or notched. If tinsel or crinkle-tie is used, the ends may be curled. To curl, press ribbon on dull knife blade and pull knife along under each piece. Odds and ends of various colors and kinds of ribbon may be combined to make effective use of leftovers.

31

a

b

c

d

Fig. 28. Poinsettia bow

a

b

c

d

Fig. 29. Hair bow

POINSETTIA BOW *(Fig. 28)*. For a medium-sized poinsettia bow, use ribbon between 2 and 3 inches wide. Use a red satin ribbon with a very crisp finish. If the ribbon is 2 inches wide, measure off with pins along selvage at 2-inch spaces the whole length of the ribbon; if 3 inches wide, the pins should be placed 3 inches apart. Next, cut across ribbon on diagonal lines to form petals as shown in illustration *(a)*.

Pinch gathers along straight grain of ribbon as indicated by dotted lines *(b)*. Hold gathers in place by twisting tightly with thread. Arrange three petals to form a six-pointed flower *(c)*. Fill in center with a knot of yellow baby ribbon or with a yellow flower center.

This type of bow will find many uses when decorating at Christmas. Also because it will lie flat, it is ideal for packages to be mailed *(d)*.

HAIR BOW *(Fig. 29)*. Place ribbon in S or double-S shape, keeping right side up *(a)*. Cover with open hand and gather ribbons together between first and second fingers *(b)*. Tie in center and attach to package *(c* and *d)*. Slip a bobby pin under loop on back of bow, then it is all ready to be worn in the hair. This is a pretty bow for any feminine gift and is especially suitable for children's packages.

WREATH BOW *(Fig. 30)*. The wreath bow requires 2½ yards of ribbon 4 or 5 inches wide. Cut the ribbon into the following lengths: 16

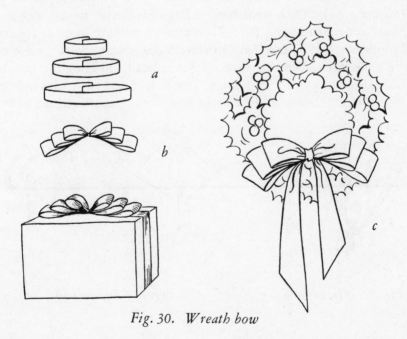

Fig. 30. Wreath bow

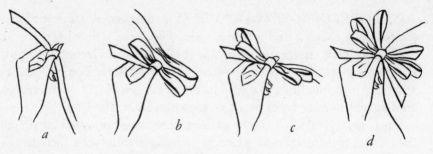

Fig. 31. Corsage bow

inches, 20 inches, and 24 inches. The 30-inch piece remaining is used for ends.

Fold ends of each piece to the center, overlap, and hold in place with two or three stitches as shown in illustration (*a*). Arrange loops in layers and pinch all centers together (*b*). Tie securely with narrow ribbon or wire. Tie the 30-inch piece around the center, knotting it in back, and allow ends to fall as streamers (*c*). You can also use only one or two loops if you prefer.

(The glamour bow [*Fig. 15*] made with only two or four loops, may also be used as a wreath bow by the addition of long streamer ends.)

CORSAGE BOW (*Fig. 31*). Hold ribbon between thumb and first finger of left hand, allowing end to extend 3 or 4 inches as shown in illustration (*a*). With right hand, bring ribbon over thumb nail and around and under thumb (*b*). Then proceed to make loops as for the glamour bow (*c*). Make ten or twelve loops. Next, insert a piece of wire under the ribbon that covers the thumbnail and bring the wire to underside of loops (*d*). Slip thumb out of loop and twist wire tightly. The center thus made on the corsage bow is its chief attraction.

Fig. 32. Greek bow

Fig. 33. Square bow

GREEK BOW *(Fig. 32).* Long ago the Greeks devised a simple arrangement of ribbon loops which is now generally used with floral decorations and is called the Greek bow.

Cut 3-inch-width (or wider) ribbon 6- or 7-inch lengths. Gather ends and bring together to form a loop. Wind with wire to hold. Allow the end of wire to extend as a stem. This makes one petal. Cover wire and base of petal with green mending tissue. (Florists have this, so do craft supply houses—any place where material for making artificial flowers is sold.) When several are combined, they make an upstanding bow that is particularly effective in baskets of flowers or potted plants.

Fig. 33. A variation of this type of bow has ends instead of loops. To make it, cut wide ninon or gauzy-type ribbon into squares. Pinch center

Fig. 34. Pussy cat bow

of square so that all edges stand upright. Twist wire tightly around pinched portion and let the wire extend to form a stem. If you place an odd bead or tiny button in the center of the square, it will be easier to twist wire around it and the wire cannot pull off. Edges may be fringed or cut with pinking shears. Changeable taffeta squares, fringed on edges make a pretty trim.

PUSSY CAT BOW *(Fig. 34).* To make this bow, cross ends over as shown in illustration (*a*). Wind center with thread or wire (*b*). If desired, center may be covered with narrow baby ribbon of matching or contrasting color and an ornament tied in (*c*).

FIGURE-8 BOW *(Fig. 35).* Work ribbon back and forth in loops in the form of a figure 8. The bow shown is made with a silver tinsel ribbon which has a firm body. You may find it easier to make the bow

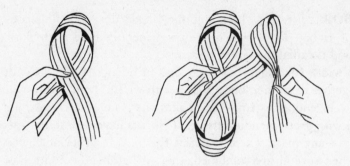

Fig. 35. Figure-8 bow

in reverse position. Turn the bow (as shown) upside down and make the figure 8 small to start with, making each one successively larger.

BASKET BOW *(Fig. 36).* Make a loop at one end of a piece of ribbon and wind with strong thread or soft fine wire (do not break thread). Make a second loop next to the first one (loops will be ½ to ¾ inch apart) and wind with same thread as used on first loop (see illustration [*a*]). As each loop is made, push it away under palm of left hand and proceed with the next one. Continue winding loops in this manner until desired number of loops has been made (about ten to fifteen). Do not cut thread yet. Now you will have a continuous row of loops. Wind them into a circle so that all stand upright. To hold them in this position, wind them together with the thread in and out between loops (*b*), then tie thread or wire and leave ends for attaching to package. This bow is particularly suitable for baskets and large packages. (P.S. For the ladies: it's nice, too, on your hat!)

TIED BOW. While tied bows are seldom used on packages, they are frequently used to trim dolls, toy animals, lingerie, etc.

Fig. 37. Place ribbon around neck or bundle of towels or other such object. First illustration: Cross right end, *A,* over left end, *B,* and draw under and up. Pull both ends to form knot. Second illustration: End *A*

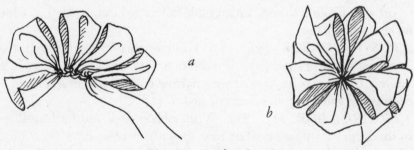

a

b

Fig. 36. Basket bow

is now up, and *B* is down. Make a loop on *B* by turning the end *up* and hold with thumb and finger of right hand. Third illustration: Bring *A* down over center and at this point make a second loop on *A*, and

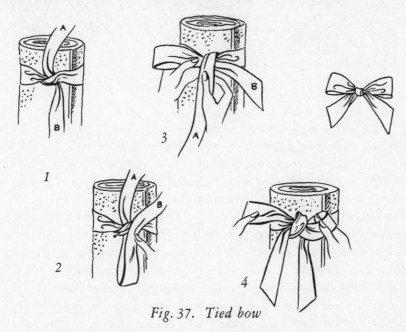

Fig. 37. *Tied bow*

push this loop through space between first loop and knot. Fourth illustration: Pull both loops to tighten, and adjust length of ends and loops. Fifth illustration: The resulting bow will have two loops at top, two ends at bottom, and a neat, smooth center.

Variation 1: pin-on bow (Fig. 38). Another type of tied bow is quickly made as follows: Use 24 inches of ribbon and make a loop 3 inches long about 3 or 4 inches from one end. Pinch gathers (*a*) and hold between thumb and finger of right hand. Pick up longer end near

Fig. 38. *Pin-on bow*

Fig. 39. Pin-on bow (Variation 2)

this point and bring it around under finger of right hand and up over fingernail (*b*), then down under the center and push with left thumb through a space between right hand fingernail and the ribbon that covers it. Catch loop thus formed with right thumb and finger as you let go of the first loop. Pull both loops to tighten knot (*c*).

Variation 2: pin-on bow (Fig. 39). Fold a half yard length of ribbon as shown in illustration (*a*). Bring end on left up over the center (*b*) and around and behind both layers of ribbon, then down. Tie both ends in a single knot. This makes a decorative twisted knot (*c*) which is particularly pretty when made with a two-tone satin ribbon. The pin-on bow is particularly suitable for sewing on lingerie, dolls' clothes, handkerchief corners, baby clothes, etc., before placing in gift box.

HOW AND WHERE TO PLACE BOWS ON THE PACKAGE

Always place the bow on the package with an eye to balance and proportion. For instance, on a square or round box, the bow will look best if placed directly in the center, but on all other shapes place bow at the side, end, or along the edge. This asymmetric line is more pleasing. Do not use a bow so large that it overpowers the package. Use big bows on big boxes, smaller bows on smaller ones. Experiment with your own ideas until you get an effect or arrangement that pleases you. There are endless possibilities. The size and position of bows on the packages illustrated in this book may be a help in guiding you.

Bows may be tied, wired, pinned, taped, or pasted to the package.

Tying or Wiring. Tie bow to box in one of the following two ways. Either place the center of the loops on the knot of the package and tie it on with the ends of the ribbon left long when tying the box (*Fig. 12*), or slide the ends of the wire or thread, with which you have wound the loops, under the ribbon already on the package and twist it under bow.

Pinning. You can pin wide ribbon bows to the box if there are no bands of ribbon onto which to tie it. Push pins slantwise through the underneath loops near the center. Use three or four pins pushed in at different angles. They will hold bow firmly and are easily removed.

Taping. Slip small pieces of Scotch tape through a few of the bottom loops near the center of the bow. Use narrow strips of tape and allow the ends to extend far enough to hold bow securely to the box.

Pasting. Flat bows are best suited for attaching to boxes in this manner. Use household cement, mucilage, or library paste and spread it lightly on the box, then place bow and loops on it. Press gently but firmly until it sets.

ADDING DECORATIVE TRIMMINGS

Many beautiful and unusual packages may be created by combining bows with other trimmings and by the use of novel arrangements. The following are a few suggestions.

Fringe both ends of a short length of ribbon (8 to 12 inches). Place the center of this strip underneath a matching bow and allow the fringed ends to extend beyond the bow. (In much the same manner as *Fig. 45,* but use one length of ribbon with two ends and a bow instead of the decoration.)

Fig. 40. Ruffle one edge of a 27-inch length of ribbon 2 or 3 inches wide and shape ruffle into a rose. This can be used instead of bow.

Shredded Ends. (Fig. 41). Plastic type highly glossed ribbon may have ends shredded by cutting into narrow strips. Place underneath the bow, allowing shredded ends to extend.

Fig. 40.
Ruffle bow

Fig. 41. Shredded ends

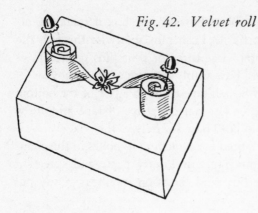

Fig. 42. Velvet roll

Fig. 43. Grosgrain roll

Velvet ribbon. *(Fig. 42).* Makes a luxurious trim when used on foil paper. It is ideal for that extra-special gift. An unusual treatment (illustrated) is to roll the ribbon from each end toward the center until there are only a few inches of space between each roll. Pin the roll to prevent unrolling. Then place a roll at each side of box center. Make one turn of ribbon at center. Stick a hatpin down through the center of each roll and add a fancy pin or small flower at the center between the rolls. In this way you won't mar the velvet and the recipient will be able to use it fashionwise after she has opened her gift.

Rolls of ribbon. *(Fig. 43).* Grosgrain ribbon can also be made into rolls. Lay the ribbon flat on the table and roll the ends toward the center. Pin on the under side to hold. Place a bright scatter pin between

Fig. 44. Ruffle trim

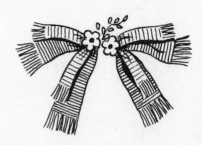

Fig. 45. Fringed trim

the rolls and you will have a little novelty that may be used on a small box and which can be worn later on a lapel.

A ribbon braid is colorful and may be used as a frame for a card or picture on a package. Hold in place with short pins pushed through lid of box. In addition to making a pretty package, it may be used later as a belt or headband.

Fig. 44. Frame a package with a ribbon ruffle. Take a piece of ribbon about 1½ to 2 inches wide and 2 yards long. Run a gathering thread lengthwise through the center and draw up to form ruffle one yard long. Pin this around the top edge of the box as a frame for a scene which is pasted on the box top.

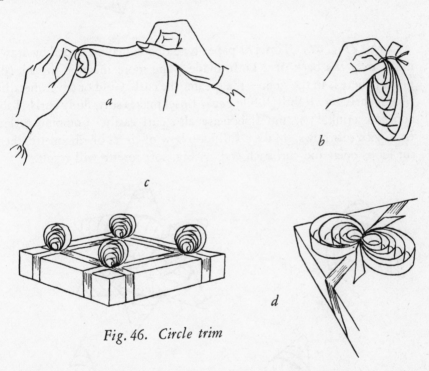

Fig. 46. *Circle trim*

Fig. 45. Short pieces of ribbon may be fringed and tied to make a trimming with a center decoration—flowers, brooch, etc.

Circle trim. (Fig. 46). Hold ribbon between thumb and finger and make loops as shown in illustrations (*a*) and (*b*). Scotch-tape these to hold. Place these loops upright on two or four corners of the package (*c*) and hold again with Scotch tape. Or lay the loops flat on package to form fancy designs (*d*). Conceal centers with a bow or spray of flowers or evergreen.

Fig. 47. Curl trim

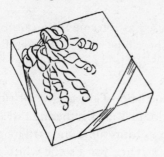

Fig. 48. Knotted trim

Curls. *(Fig. 47).* Tinsel or paper-type ribbon may be curled by drawing it over the back of a knife blade. The more metallic thread (or paper) there is in the ribbon, the greater the curl. Gold or silver metallic ribbon curls very tightly, while gauzy tinsel makes soft, fluffy curls. Ribbonzene, crinkle-tie, and ribbonette also curl easily. Combine curled ends with soft bows. Make a full loop bow of tinsel or ribbonette, then cut loops open and curl each end. A big, soft rosette will result.

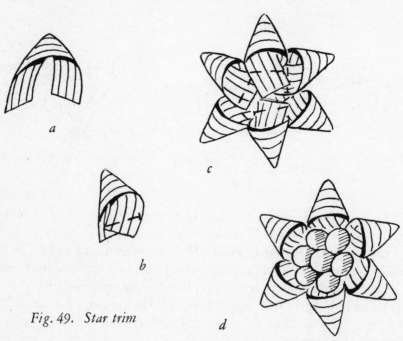

a

b

c

d

Fig. 49. Star trim

Knotted trim. (Fig. 48). Tie a knot in the center of short lengths of ribbon and pin or tape to package. This is a good way to use up odds and ends.

Star trim. (Fig. 49). Use 1½-inch-width ribbon. Cut 4-inch pieces (*a*) and fold in funnel shape by lapping ends to form petals (*b*). Arrange petals to form a star and stitch ends together (*c*). This is novel on packages and also makes a pretty place card at a party table. It may be filled with candy (*d*) or ornaments.

The Christmas Package

Christmas, of course, surpasses all other occasions for gift-wrapping activity, and the possibilities for making attractive packages are endless. The religious and popular traditions of the season as well as the time of year, provide as varied a choice of motifs as anyone could wish. All kinds of designs are available in printed paper, seals, or tags; and it is a matter of personal taste what theme, color scheme, and type of design you select. In southern or tropical climates, where Christmas Day is like a northern midsummer day, there is further choice of suitable motifs and colors.

Naturally, in selecting wrapping material for presents that you are giving to a wide group of people at Christmas, it is well to take into account their age and taste as well as your own. Some papers and seals are appropriate for young children and not for adults, and vice versa. Also, if your friend is sophisticated, don't wrap his or her gift in a cute or sentimental paper—use plain colors or a stylish modern design. Plain or striped papers and ribbons are always safe for everyone and usually the most simple and artistic effects are achieved with them. If you know your friend's favorite color, use it, or try to remember the type of decoration and colors in his or her house or apartment, or use your own favorite colors, as an expression of yourself. But keep off pink or feminine colors for your gift to a man or boy.

Of course, many printed papers come in attractive designs, and varying the wrappings as much as possible adds interest under the Christmas tree. On principle, *don't* mix design ribbons with design papers. If you select a traditional holly-design printed paper, for instance, use a plain-colored ribbon, such as red, or if the paper is multicolored, use a plain-colored ribbon such as white, yellow, gold, silver, green or blue, whichever looks best with the colors of the paper you have chosen. If you use plain-colored paper, you can use a striped or decorated ribbon instead of a plain one and you might tie or tape your Christmas card onto the package itself to give it a gay effect, or stick on two or three silver or gold stars of appropriate size. You can also attach fir cones, bells, or a sprig of artificial mistletoe or holly to the center of the ribbon or bow. Don't overdo it though; that is, don't choose a "busy" looking paper and a patterned ribbon and add different seals, bells, or other unrelated decorations on top of this. It's always in better taste to do the simple. Only add a touch of ornament where you have a relatively plain background which will show up that ornament to advantage.

Another *don't:* avoid mixing themes. If you decide on a religious theme, keep to the nativity, stars, bells, candles, etc. Don't add Santa Claus seals or mistletoe. Or, if you decide on Santa Claus as a theme for paper or seals, don't add the religious theme in your stickers. The main themes for Christmas follow, with a few suggestions for each type of wrapping.

If you wish to stress *family ties and the traditional Christmas spirit,* your theme centers around fireside scenes, chimneys, Santa with his reindeer and bag of toys, Christmas trees, wreaths, yule logs, gifts and gift stockings, children, and other designs centering about family life and activities. Or you may use plain, bright colors that look gay and festive.

If you choose fun and gaiety as your theme, choose paper or decorations depicting snow scenes and evergreens, skaters, skiers, sledders, sleigh bells, animals, mistletoe and holly.

If the *religious story* is your choice, your papers and decorations should reflect this with stars, bells, glowing candles, churches and church bells, choir boys, angels, wise men, shepherds, manger scenes, and the many other designs that have religious significance. Again, don't overdo it. Pick one or, at the most, two of such designs in paper or stickers. The most effective packages are simple. Plain paper with just one seal or card or accessory to express the theme you have chosen is all that is necessary.

You may decide that *color* is your theme and do up all your packages in the same color so that several packages to one family will be easily identified as coming from you. For this you might use plain paper and ribbon, or wrap with two colored papers (half and half) and cover the join with your ribbon. Or, in place of color, choose one particular de-

Opposite page: Miscellaneous Christmas wrappings

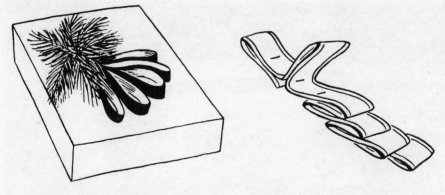

Fig. 50. *Ribbon loops*   Fig. 51. *Stapled loops*

sign that you really like for all boxes (bells, stars, stripes, etc.) to individualize your gifts. You may wish to use the same ribbon for all your gifts—or the same type of bow, seals, card, Christmas bouquet—as a stamp of your own personality. Your choice is practically limitless. Another advantage to this idea is that you can buy a large quantity of one sort of paper or ribbon at less cost than a mixed assortment of small pieces and short lengths of tying material.

TRIMMING THE CHRISTMAS PACKAGE

Any of the bows shown in the preceding section can, of course, be used on your Christmas packages and, in addition, you will find a number of trimming suggestions in the following paragraphs.

Fig. 50. Ribbon loops falling from underneath a sprig of pine make an effective trim. The loops should be uneven in length and made to go in one direction. Fasten together with a pin and tape to the package.

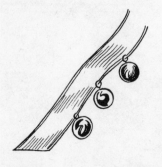

Fig. 52. *Ornaments on ribbon*

Fig. 53. *End trimming*

Then add a sprig or two of pine to cover loop ends, and tape or pin this in place. Evergreens may be tucked in or under any red bow for extra glamour. Poinsettias, Christmas seals, snow, white branches, (see notes page 49 on how to make these) and scores of other novelty trimmings and ribbons make your packages interesting.

Fig. 51. Small flat loops may be quickly stapled so that each succeeding loop covers the staple underneath. This makes a pretty trim when placed along one edge of a package or as a cascade underneath a bow.

Fig. 52. You can use *Christmas tree ornaments* to decorate the ends of a wide ribbon bow along one side. Remove cotter pin from top of ornament. Push one end of cotter pin through edge of ribbon and then push both ends back into the ornament.

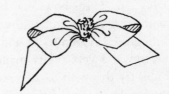

Fig. 55.   Decorated bow

Fig. 54.   Scarf ring trim

Fig. 53. A cluster of bells, berries, or tiny ornaments can be tied in with a bow at one end of a narrow ribbon to hang loose on a package. It can also be tied firm as a centerpiece.

Sew a bit of *narrow white lace* along one edge of a piece of red ribbon, then loop into a bow. This gives a flattering feminine quality to the ribbon and the package.

Any number of other ideas may be developed to create pretty packages that are unusual. In *Fig. 54,* for instance, the ends of tying ribbon are pulled through a *scarf ring.* Here are a few other ideas with which you may wish to experiment.

Two big gold or silver *hat pins* may be used to decorate a knot.

Small *bottles of perfume* may be tied on ends of narrow ribbon.

Scatter pins will decorate ribbon bands. *Earrings* can be clamped on bow centers (*Fig. 55*).

Fig. 56.   Fig. 57.

Decorated bows

A few *sequins* may be touched with glue and placed on ribbon or box.
Fig. 56. Large bows may be enhanced by the addition of *tiny bows* in contrasting color. In the illustration narrow white baby ribbon is slipped through red ribbon loops and tied in tiny bows. This causes the loop to puff up in a very pretty manner and the color contrast is showy. You might try this with narrow red ribbon on wide silver tinsel bows, or use narrow gold tinsel on green satin bows. A variation of this idea is shown in *Fig. 57.* Tiny bows are placed on top of loops for a new note of interest.

"Glitter" effects. After a bow is made, brush loops and ends lightly with a bit of mucilage and sprinkle with flitter (a tinsel dust which comes in small bottles and in a choice of many colors—at artist's supply stores or wrapping-paper counters). Names, initials, stars, or any design you care to make can be lightly traced on the ribbon or package with mucilage, and then the flitter can be sprinkled over the mucilage lines for the desired effect. Small branches or bare twigs may also be decorated with flitter or mica snow flakes and used on packages. Instructions on how to do this follow.

How to make starched branches for winter bouquets. (1) Mix 2 tablespoons of laundry starch to a smooth paste with a little cold water. Add boiling water, stirring rapidly to a creamy consistency. If it is too thick, add more water. Into this mixture dip bare branches, wild flower stalks, seed pods, or various evergreens except those with long needles like pine. Shake off excess moisture and quickly dip branch into Christmas mica or snow which has been scattered over sheets of newspaper. Put in vases to dry for several hours. Then arrange.

How to make white branches. To color ornamental branches white, mix 2 cups of cornstarch and 1 cup of flour with enough cold water to make a rather syrupy paste. Select your twig branches and dip into mixture. Place on paper until thoroughly dry.

Make a gay *border* by pasting Christmas seals around the four sides of the top of a package.

Cut out a colorful *picture* or *design* from gift paper or a magazine and paste in the center of your gift-wrapped box. Frame picture with ½-inch-wide ribbon pasted in place.

Use a colorful little *basket box* as a container for candies, sewing material, or some other small gift like the example in the center of the color frontispiece. Place a brooch, a spray of flowers, a Christmas ornament, or a bow on the top. The little basket is a gift in itself.

Christmas gifts for children may be packaged in the ever-popular *Christmas stocking.*

Paper made to look like *fireplace brick* is fun for wrapping a doll's house or large box. Red oilcloth is also good—and afterward it can be cut into place mats, used to cover play cushions, or used on shelves in the playroom.

See the chapter on wrapping gifts for children for additional ideas that may be adapted for Christmas time.

The Selection and Decoration of Gifts for Special Occasions

It may be comparatively easy to decide on a present for someone at Christmas or for a birthday because these happen every year and you know the kind of presents you like to give and that have been most appreciated in the past. But there are many other occasions when you are suddenly called upon to make some flattering gesture and you are not sure what sort of thing is right to give. It is with this in mind that half of this chapter has been written. Every occasion likely to occur is listed with gift suggestions and, in each case, this is followed by ideas for suitable types of wrapping as in the rest of the book. At the end of this chapter there is a list of special days in the year on which gifts are customarily given—and days that have a special significance in case some personal gift should be presented at any of these times and you like the idea of using the theme of the day for your colors or trimmings.

Before choosing a present, spend some time thinking about the person you are going to give it to, and consider his or her personality, taste, or needs. You will, of course, also be guided by the amount you are prepared to spend. The gift suggestions made here for anniversaries, babies, birthdays, bon voyage, Easter, Father's Day, Mother's Day, mourning, graduation, holidays, hostesses, invalids, prizes, showers, Valentine's Day, Thanksgiving, and the New Year are given merely as a stimulus to your own thinking and are, *of course,* not to be considered as the only answers to your gift-giving problems. There are a few do's and don'ts, however, that everyone should know.

Very often it is necessary—or appropriate—to give one gift to a family as a whole. Or two or more gifts may be given to the same individual. The latter, for convenience, is referred to as a *multiple gift.* When several people "chip in" to give someone a present, this has been called a *group gift.* Suggestions for such gifts and their wrappings are given later in this chapter.

Be on time. This is the first *do.* When a gift is called for, it should arrive on the appointed day, or better still, a day or so ahead of time. There is nothing quite so anticlimactic as to receive a gift several days after the occasion for which it was intended. Keep a record of dates to be remembered so that you can purchase gifts and allow plenty of time for delivery.

Keep gifts on hand. The wise person buys an attractive object when he sees it at a favorable price and keeps this for some future gift occasion. This way you can save last-minute rushes and disappointment at not getting just what you want.

ANNIVERSARIES

The anniversary celebration has become an established custom. The occasion for celebration may be the date of someone's birth, the date you met someone very special, the date you got the new job or moved into a new home. However, with the exception of birthdays, the wedding anniversary is the one most often celebrated, and for at least the first five years many young couples receive from their family and friends gifts or cards commemorating the event.

The first anniversary gifts are of paper. If you wish to abide by this tradition, there are many useful and attractive items which make very acceptable gifts. There are stationery sets, books, magazines (subscriptions), reproductions of paintings (printed on paper), notebooks, paper towels, bridge or luncheon sets, picnic supplies, monographed match books, cedar bags, a hat box, gift-wrapping sets, and so on.

Wrapping suggestions. White or pastel papers tied with paper or plastic ribbon to match or contrast. (Ideas for magazine subscriptions appear on page 81.) Trims: paper flowers or bells, paper dolls, fans of pleated paper or doilies Scotch-taped on top of the wrapping. If you are clever in this direction, cut up paper, make a flower and stick it on top.

Two different ways of wrapping a book (instructions, page 19).

The second anniversary calls for gifts of cotton. Your choice might be a quilt, cushions, curtains, sheets, towels, fabrics, slip covers, bedspreads, or any other item from a long list of cotton goods.

Wrapping suggestions. Use paper or cotton cloth and decorate with ball fringe, braid, cotton balls, etc.

The third anniversary calls for leather. Here the choice of gifts extends to luggage, desk sets, slippers, gloves, purses, belts, brief cases, photograph frames, a leather-bound dictionary or book, leather-covered wastepaper basket or clothes brush, and so on.

Wrapping suggestions. Leather-colored paper (maroon, brown, or pigskin shade) tied with kid-white or brown moire ribbon, leather shoe strings or, if you like, a leather belt—an additional gift in itself. Decorate with key-tainer, leather-covered buttons, or patent leather flowers or novelties in all leather colors.

The fourth anniversary gifts should be made of silk. Scarfs, handkerchiefs, hosiery, dressing gowns, silk embroidery or tapestry, a blouse, fabric for household coverings (bed, cushions, drapes, etc.), are a few ideas.

Wrapping suggestions. Wrap the gift in silk, or in extra-fine tissue paper. Tie with silk ribbon. Decorate with silk bows, silk fringe, silk tassels, or paste scraps of silk on the package in patchwork quilt fashion.

For the fifth anniversary, the appropriate material for gifts is wood. The wide selection includes inexpensive items such as a salad bowl, bread board, book ends, or more elaborate pieces like furniture, a piece of wood sculpture, a birdhouse, antique decoy duck (on its own as a decorative piece or as a lamp base), and so on.

Wrapping suggestions. Brown paper, cedar lining paper cut from a cedar closet bag, or a wood-grained wallpaper or gift paper. Tie with moire ribbon. For added novelty, decorate package with wooden spoons, coasters, colored toothpicks, or clothespins.

The tenth anniversary is traditionally tin. These gift customs were established long before the manufacture of aluminum articles, and today gifts made of either tin or aluminum are appropriate. The wide variety of both items on the market makes selection easy—all the way from pots and pans to decorative tin objects and trays, like those made in Mexico, or antique American painted boxes, pin trays, watering cans, etc.

Wrapping suggestions. Tin foil, aluminum foil, or any of the metallic papers. Tie with metallic ribbon. Possible additional decorations: tin spoons, small aluminum cooking equipment (measuring spoons, cookie cutters, jelly molds), tin cups, simple small tools or toys, tin soldiers, or a tin horn.

The fifteenth anniversary is crystal. Any glassware or gift department has a wide selection of beautiful table glassware and vases from which to make a selection. Antique shops are, of course, a good source for old chandeliers, goblets, bowls, paperweights, vases, painted glass, and more expensive gifts. Then there are glass-bead necklaces, shirt studs, etc.

Wrapping suggestions. Wrap such gifts very carefully, using plenty of shredded paper or excelsior to prevent breakage. Use pale blue metallic paper, cellophane, or clear plastic for box coverings. Tie with gauzy tinsel ribbon or any of the laminated ribbons that look like glass.

Other decorative touches: Sprinkle silver flitter on the bows and on the package itself to make it sparkle like crystal (see "Trimming the Christmas Package" for information on use of mucilage and flitter). Decorate with a bunch of cellophane glassips (straws), gather at center by wire, with ends spreading out in ball shape, or with cellophane or glass flowers, glass spoons, beads, or rhinestone brooch.

The twentieth anniversary focuses attention on the china closet. Here again there are thousands of beautiful pieces to choose from. You may wish to fill in an old set of china, buy a new dinnerware or breakfast set, or find odd articles such as vases, lamps, bowls, platters, antique porcelain figurines, table centerpieces, etc.

Wrapping suggestions. Because the name "china," as well as the techniques for producing it, is associated with the country of China, it may prove amusing to wrap your gift to show this influence. Plain white or cream wrapping paper may be colorfully painted with Chinese characters. Embossed foil or printed papers with Chinese motifs may be used. Or you may prefer plain papers in colors popularly associated with the Chinese: peacock blue, jade green, Mandarin red, or mustard yellow. Tie with contrasting ribbons of the same colors (red on green or yellow paper; or yellow ribbon on blue or green paper, etc.) You can also use fluorescent ribbon. For additional effect, you might pleat the ribbon into fan shapes; tie on a miniature china doll, figurine, flowers, a piece of Chinese embroidery; or paste on the top a reproduction from a Chinese scroll painting—if you can find one in a museum, picture shop—or from an art magazine.

The twenty-fifth (silver) anniversary is cause for a real celebration. Modern or antique silver tableware, ornaments, or jewelry should be carefully selected for this event and the wrapping should receive as much attention as the gift itself.

Wrapping suggestions. Silver paper or aluminum foil, or place the gift in a mirror-covered box. Trim with silver or white satin ribbon. If money is to be the gift, you can glue silver coins on cardboard to form the numerals "25" and frame as a picture or glue them in a random design. Packages or bows may be decorated with silver bells, pins, rings, beads, bracelets, silver novelties, or a spray of white flowers, always suitable for any anniversary occasion.

The fiftieth anniversary is, of course, gold. The occasion of a *golden wedding anniversary,* because of its rarity, is usually marked by a large reunion of the family and old family friends. Gifts of gold may be

jewelry, pen and pencil set, gold leaf picture frames, gold-plate tableware (somewhat rare). Then there are gold-trimmed china and glassware from which to make a selection. The "golden" theme may also be
expressed through the use of gold as a color only. Golden-yellow linen,
gold silk or wool damask, gold brocades, etc., are all possibilities.

Wrapping suggestions. This anniversary naturally calls for the use of
gold or yellow paper and ribbons, with gold trinkets or yellow flowers
as decoration. Don't wrap and tie the package all in one shade. If you
want an all-gold effect, vary the shades of gold paper and ribbon; use
yellow ribbons on gold paper or vice versa, or a light gold ribbon on a
dark gold paper; or use gold-and-white striped paper, or moss-green or
rose for a second ribbon under the gold one, so the package is not
monotonous.

BABY GIFTS

Since a baby's arrival has been anticipated for some months, its initial
wardrobe is usually quite complete, so it is a good plan to choose items
of clothing in sizes *large enough* for the baby to grow into. Soft sweaters,
blankets, dresses, bibs, rompers—blue for a boy, pink for a girl, and
pale yellow or white for either are gifts all mothers will welcome.

Wrapping suggestions. The gift wrapping for a baby's present should
be in keeping with the gift: the colors soft; the design dainty; the ribbon
of pastel colors, often made into small rosettes which may be used later
on bootees or bonnets if desired. Special printed papers, ribbons, and
seals are available for the occasion at stores that sell wrapping papers;
or, if you want to be different, paste different plain-colored paper on
each of the sides of a square box (to resemble a building block) and
decorate with the baby's initials. If the package is large, a bassinet bow,
to be used later, will be a most welcome decoration.

Decorate a baby's package with a rattle, teething ring, soap babies,
tiny cans of talcum powder, powder puff, soft wash cloth or any other
small practical thing that the mother can use for her new charge.

BIRTHDAYS

Much depends on how well you know the person whose birthday you
wish to remember. If in the family and you know exactly what he or she
wants (and you can afford the price) the question is automatically
settled, as for any other occasion. In this book it is possible to discuss
appropriate types of presents only in very general terms. For birthdays,

The package at right is of quilted pink paper. The age numerals are of flitter sprinkled on glue base. (See page 48 under "flitter effects.")

however, birthstones set in rings, bracelets, necklaces, earrings, tie pins, dress shirt studs, or cuff links make good lifetime gifts. Stones and flowers associated with the various months are:

Month	Birthstone	Flower
January	garnet	snowdrop
February	amethyst	primrose
March	bloodstone	violet
April	diamond	lily
May	emerald	lily of the valley
June	pearl	rose
July	ruby	sweet pea
August	sardonyx	gladiola
September	sapphire	aster
October	opal	dahlia
November	topaz	chrysanthemum
December	turquoise	holly

Books, too, are never amiss as inexpensive birthday presents, and, if a good choice is made each year, a valuable basic library may result—or be added to. A wrist watch is also excellent for adolescent boys or girls, a

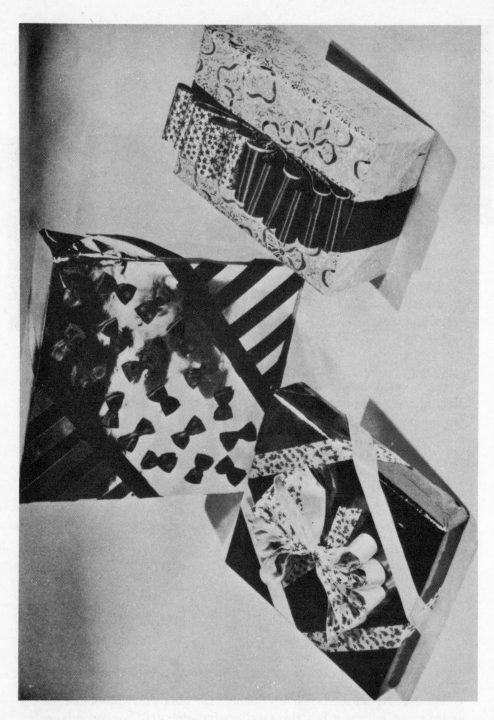

pen and pencil set, candies, victrola records (provided that you know the taste of the individual and what equipment he or she has). Then there is luggage to consider, or else something for the house in the case of a newlywed. A diary makes an inexpensive appropriate birthday gift for a girl. And, of course, all types of clothing and accessories are always welcome. In the latter case, better make sure the store will change the gift if it is the wrong size or color.

Those who have a garden, where a plant, tree, or shrub would enhance some corner, will enjoy watching such a gift grow year after year and will remember you for it. (The florist or nursery will tell you what is in season for planting.) See page 82 for suggestions on wrapping and presenting this type of gift.

Wrapping suggestions. You will find a wide variety of papers, ribbons, cards, and seals designed specifically for birthday presents. Plain papers and ribbons tied in any kind of bow (see chapter on How to Wrap Your Gift) are always right. For hot months use cool colors, for the cold months use warmer ones. For sheer nonsense you can wrap the gift in a page torn from a large calendar. Arrange the page on the package so the numerals come on top—and circle the birth date in red. You can trim a birthday package with large "lucky" stars cut from silver paper— or get stickers of this shape. Imitation birthstones or the birth flower are excellent decorations.

Another interesting decorative theme for a birthday gift might be built around the *zodiac* sign. Some of these signs lend themselves better than others. You can cut a design from some magazine, or trace it from a book you may own or get some toy replica such as a bull (Taurus), fish (Pisces), lion (Leo), crab (Cancer), etc., either in costume jewelry or in the form of a toy.* The following list shows dates with corresponding signs:

March 21—April 19, Aries (Ram)
April 20—May 20, Taurus (Bull)
May 21—June 21, Gemini (Twins)
June 22—July 22, Cancer (Crab)
July 23—August 23, Leo (Lion)
August 24—September 23, Virgo
 (Virgin)
September 24—October 23, Libra
 (Scales)

October 24—November 22, Scorpio
 (Scorpion)
November 23—December 21,
 Sagittarius (Archer)
December 22—January 19, Capricorn
 (Sea Goat)
January 20—February 18, Aquarius
 (Water Carrier)
February 19—March 20, Pisces
 (Fishes)

* An attractive set of post cards has been made of each sign by the Museum of Natural History, New York.

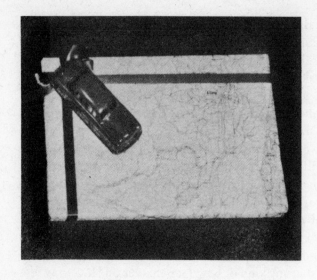

A package wrapped in a road map with toy plastic car tied at corner. (See below.)

BON VOYAGE

When a friend is going on a holiday or on an extended trip, the air is charged with anticipation, and any gift, however small, adds to the happy excitement. In choosing such a gift, consider carefully the problem of luggage, and *never* give anything to complicate it. Rather choose something to add to the gaiety and pleasure of the trip. A corsage, attractively boxed by the florist, is proof to one's fellow travelers that thoughtful friends were left behind. Books, magazines, a basket of food, candy, film for the camera (provided you know the kind and size of camera), a gaily wrapped notebook are ideal. When the good-byes to family and friends are over and the traveler is on his way, there is nothing more heartwarming than to open a package, be it serious, beautiful, or nonsensical, and read the affectionate notes enclosed with the gifts. If you take a picture of the departure, you can give it later as a surprise birthday or Christmas gift.

Wrapping suggestions. Wrap the gift in bon voyage paper, or wrap with a road map, a timetable, or plain paper decorated with cut-out scenes from travel maps, posters, or advertisements of the country or place where your friend is going. Tie with colorful ribbon. You could also trim the package with travel stickers like a piece of well-traveled and much loved luggage. (See photograph above and page 76, top right.)

58

FATHER'S DAY

This is a day for giving Father a gift designed or chosen especially for him. Give something very personal for which he has expressed a desire. And then take care not to charge it on an account for which he will have to pay in the end!

A bedside radio (if there's not already too much noise in the house), an adjustable bed lamp that will shed light only on his book, a new pen and pencil or desk set, suitcase, electric razor, pipe, humidor, shoe trees, slippers, bathrobe, cigarette lighter, a gadget for his car, a technical or sports book in which he is interested, seeds, plants, a tool for the garden. The family will know best what he most needs and would enjoy.

Wrapping suggestions. The wrapping of father's gift is very important. He will appreciate the trouble you take to make his gift appealing and individual. No doubt he will enjoy a little teasing, too, so you might wrap his gift in a box of proper size, then nest it into a larger box, and finally into a still larger one. Wrap each box as if it were the one containing the gift, so that he will have the fun and suspense of undoing three or four packages before actually finding his gift. If children are watching, they too will enjoy it a lot. Use paper that is suitably masculine, and decorate in a novel manner. Get a blank telegram, write an appropriate message on it, and paste on top of the package. Or wrap

A sophisticated package in black and white, with layer bow (page 30)

the package in a sheet of popular music, the sentiment and words of which fit the occasion. Tie ribbon around the package in the form of a four-in-hand tie, or hook a bow tie around the box. Many papers and ribbons are designed expressly for men and you may make your selection from among these—or use plain brown or red or the color you know he likes best, with contrasting or matching ribbon. Decorate the lid with colored scenes cut from sports magazines or cover a box with his newspaper and tie with a bright red ribbon. But perhaps the best decoration of all is a good family photo which he can later keep in his wallet.

EASTER

The Easter gift should be in keeping with the season. Flowers are always welcome; as are bulbs, seeds, and plants, if your friend has a garden. Fine perfumes, lacy blouses, lingerie, handkerchiefs, scarves are also typical Easter presents. A lovely basket filled with fruit and decorated with bows, is an attractive as well as a useful gift (see photograph, page 85). For men, a new tie, scarf, shirt, handkerchiefs, a wallet, or pair of gloves are practical gifts. For children: Easter egg candies, toy animals, books or a hobby gift to keep them occupied when the egg hunt is over.

Wrapping suggestions. Decorate Easter packages with colors symbolic of the season: purple, yellow, soft green, orchid, or any of the tulip colors. Ombré ribbon is effective. Make your bows big, puffy, and glamorous. Tuck flowers in the center of the bows, or decorate the package with an artificial flower or fruit corsage. You might wrap the box in hat veiling, add a flower or pretty ribbon bow pinned on with one or two ornamental hat pins, and you will have the trimming for an Easter bonnet right on the package. Or decorate with Easter egg dyes, packets of flower seeds, lace paper doilies, colored handkerchiefs, and, for children, with tiny chicks, bunnies, toy car, or small packet of colored candy.

MOTHER'S DAY

This day set apart to honor Mother is the occasion for giving her something strictly personal. Don't give a coffee pot, cookbook, or kitchen towels. Perhaps the best gift would be a ticket for a vacation trip or

Opposite page: Boxes wrapped in appropriate styles for Easter, Mother's Day, weddings, birthdays. The fluffy ribbon is Lacelon. (See page 11.)

61

visit she has longed to make, or two tickets to a play. A wide selection of personal items makes the choice of such a gift easy. However, a folding umbrella, engraved stationery, pinking shears, a rose bush for her garden, an attractive brooch or clip, an ornament for the house that you know she would like are all good presents with which to surprise her.

Wrapping suggestions. Wrap her gift lovingly, in materials of finest quality. Select the colors which you know are her favorites. Wrap box and lid separately so that she can open her gift without untrimming the package. She will enjoy it for days later. As for decoration—the basket design (center back) of the group of packages in the color frontispiece of this book is especially appropriate for a Mother's Day gift. You can also use a big bright bow to trim her package; or you might decorate the top of the box with her initials, adding a lacy handkerchief, a tiny bottle of perfume, small sachets, a corsage, a copy of a favorite poem, or a scarf or glove ring fastened to the center of the ribbon bow (see *Fig. 54*).

GRADUATION

All boys and girls look forward to their graduation day—whether from grammar school, high school, or college. It is an important milestone in life and deserves the kind of gift that will be long remembered and associated with the event. A few gifts of lasting value that are in keeping with the occasion are a set of books (classical stories, philosophy, biography, or poetry), book ends, a painting or a piece of sculpture, a Bible, a watch, a rosary, camera, piece of luggage, tennis racket, or any item which may prove helpful in future professional or business life. I would suggest, on this particular occasion, *not* giving clothes, candies, novelties, or anything of a transient nature. My grandmother, for instance, gave me a handmade patchwork quilt which I have always cherished.

Wrapping suggestions. Use gay papers, and tie the package with ribbons in the school colors. A list of college colors will be found at the back of this book. Roll a separate paper to resemble a diploma and tie to one streamer end. Or make a tiny book of the gift-wrapping paper, write a message inside, and tie to package or trim with mortar board. Decorate the package with a tiny lamp (to light the future path), a toy ladder (to reach the top), rose-colored glasses (sun glasses or plain ones painted with nail polish). Or you may make a big bow and tie in several extra pieces to make long ends. To each of these ends attach a knick-knack that has a symbolic meaning: for luck, a wishbone, a tiny horse-shoe (cut from cardboard); for protection from harm or evil, a rabbit's foot; for happiness, a blue bird—anything you think will amuse or touch him.

HOLIDAYS

Many birthdays coincide with holidays; and, when they do, it is fitting to acknowledge this by a special wrapping of the gift. For many of these holidays there are attractive ready-made novelties. Red, white, and blue ribbon, also paper in one or all three colors, for instance, are suitable for national holidays. Also, you will find gift paper and printed ribbons available in stores all the year round which will answer for *any* occasion and it is good to have stock of such paper on hand. (A list of national holidays and other special days appears on page 72.)

Trim packages with artificial seasonal fruit or flowers, in garlands perhaps, or use snappers, poker chips, or any novelties which suggest a gala or festive occasion. If the birthday falls on Christmas Day, or near Christmas, it is better to choose a distinguishing paper and trim that does not look like Christmas. Your gift will then stand out as a remembrance of the occasion for which it is intended.

YOUR HOSTESS

The type of gift you give your hostess depends somewhat on how well you know her. If you are in doubt as to what she would like, *do not* take a gift with you, except perhaps a small box of candy, but wait until you have completed your visit. During your stay, keep your eyes and ears open and you will learn of something that will be a happy solution to your gift problem. A book on flower arrangements, a vase or piece of pottery, candlesticks, book ends, place mats, or perhaps something more personal such as a pretty apron, scarf, or gloves—these are just a few of the many items appropriate for hostess gifts.

Wrapping suggestions. Wrap the gift with due regard for your host-ess's personality and taste which you have observed while a guest in her home. To wrap the gift you might use dull finish wallpaper, soft colors in ribbon, a single rose for a trim. Or you can do just the opposite and use gay paper with polka dot or modern design perhaps, and tie with crisp taffeta ribbon. You will have observed the colors and type of decoration she favors during your stay.

THE INVALID

The purpose of giving a present to someone confined to bed is to cheer, comfort, and entertain. *Do not give food or candy* unless you are sure that the invalid can eat it. Remember, too, that space is limited, so choose small items. You might give toilet water, an assortment of ribbons for the hair, picture magazines, manicure set, crossword puzzle book, cards for solitaire, a book of poetry, a mystery story or a novel, flowers, plant (Japanese garden), a small radio, a bath-powder mitt, toilet soap. The choice of a gift should, of course, be governed by the age and sex of the patient, the length and severity of the illness, and whether he or she is at home or in a hospital.

Wrapping suggestions. Use cheerful paper on the package and tie with gay ribbon. Polka-dot design, flower design, ombré colors, tiny dots on white background are especially good, or any of the colored fluorescent ribbons may be used. Whatever your choice of ribbon or paper, give your gift a personal touch and let your choice of gift, and the care with which you wrap it, show that you have given it both time and thought.

FOR THOSE IN MOURNING

Many a festive holiday is suddenly halted by tragedy, and one is confronted with the problem of what to do with the gift already planned. Be guided by common sense and good taste. If the gift is not appropriate at the time, keep it for a later date. In its stead extend an invitation to dinner or for a drive in the country. Give some delicacy to eat, a book, handkerchief, perfume, or other small remembrance that is sure to be appreciated. If the gift you have planned is appropriate, give it by all means and make it as attractive as you can for it will serve as an expression of your affection and sympathy.

Wrapping suggestions. Never wrap such gifts in black or even tie with black ribbon. On the other hand, too much color or gaiety is in poor taste. Keep to plain colors, neither too bright nor too somber. A white paper with a brown or dark green ribbon or the reverse might be appropriate.

An economical package tied with Ribbonette. (See page 11.)
The twisted edge loop bow is described on page 29, Fig. 22.

SHOWERS

The announcement of a girl's engagement is usually the occasion for many happy parties and much gift giving. Since your gift will be presented along with others, make the wrapping a conversation piece and select a gift that is not likely to be thought of by anyone else. Although towels, kitchen utensils, etc., are useful enough gifts and always welcome, the unusual item will probably be appreciated much more, for there is less chance of duplication. A lazy susan, a silent butler, a steam iron, napkin rings, a colorful print, a wood carving or engraving for the new home, a good cookbook, a card or coffee table, a vase or tray should prove most acceptable.

Wrapping suggestions. For decoration, there are the traditional symbols of the parasol, sprinkling pot, love birds. Use paper printed especially for this purpose: delicate floral designs or pastel-tinted plain papers. Satin ribbons, filmy gauze ribbon, or ribbon printed with appropriate patterns or sayings are in order. Make the bows big and beautiful, since the gifts will be on display and opened before a group of people. Half the fun and excitement of any party is looking at, then opening beautiful packages.

PRIZES

The winner of a prize at a party is always surrounded by envious friends who wait eagerly to see what is inside. As at a shower, the package will be the center of attraction and should be wrapped with this thought in mind. Make use of the most brilliant metallic papers, and choose a ribbon that will harmonize. Red, white, and blue striped ribbon is commonly available and is appropriate for all political or national festivities such as the Fourth of July. For school affairs, use the school colors. At bridge parties let the season be the theme—white and pastel shades for summer; orange, red, and yellow for fall; and bright contrasts like red and green through the winter. Floral ribbons, picot-edge ribbons, or moire ribbons are unusual, and done up with big glamorous bows will help to make your package a prize in itself.

THANKSGIVING DAY

Besides being a day for giving thanks, Thanksgiving is also a day of feasting. Those who are fortunate enough to have a well-stocked larder will have no difficulty in finding something to give away. In addition to food, however, beautiful linen, china, candlesticks, place mats, flowers, or table decorations are suitable gifts.

Wrapping suggestions. Baskets are fine containers for the gift of fruit, nuts, poultry, and other foods. Autumn-colored paper and ribbons should be used on packages. For decoration, there are autumn leaves and berries, chrysanthemums, a wish bone, etc. Cornucopias, the symbol of plenty, may be made from small squares of gift paper and pasted to the box.

VALENTINE'S DAY

Love birds, the activity of cupid and his bow and arrow, tiny red hearts are traditional expressions of this happy holiday. Gifts of candy, flowers, and perfume are the custom, but if something different is preferred, let it be very personal, or dainty.

Wrapping suggestions. The gift package may be wrapped with plain white tissue paper. Write an appropriate message on notepaper or card, or attach a sonnet with a red seal to the package. A big red bow, with or without a tiny cupid attached, might be just the right finishing touch. Or make a large red heart cut out of stiff paper or cardboard. Make short slits near top and bottom of heart and run a piece of ribbon through the slits. Add short extra pieces of ribbon for arrow points and head. Or paste small red hearts or tiny Valentine candies on top or ends of package. A lovely Valentine touch is to tie a single red rose, real or artificial, into the ribbon bow. You could add bluebirds cut from gift cards and paste them on plain wrapping paper. Plain paper of soft blue or rose tied with veil material in fluffy bows with flowers in the center are in the best of feminine taste.

A package suggestion for New Year's with polka-dot paper. The glamour bow used on this and many other packages illustrated is described on p. 25.

NEW YEAR'S DAY

As it comes so close to Christmas, New Year's is much less of an occasion for present giving. However, sometimes you forget someone at Christmas or the gift you ordered arrived too late for you to deliver, and the New Year provides a good occasion to send it. Also, in the usual way, there are week-end presents and special parties which often call for some gesture on the part of guests. At New Year's, any present is in order, according to the particular occasion and the personalities involved.

Wrapping suggestions. Much should be made of midnight blue and sparkling trim. A gay looking package could be wrapped in polka dot paper (see photograph, page 67). Use silver, white, green, red; or use cellophane ribbon which also has sparkle. Trim the package with a rhinestone brooch, flitter or confetti (glued on), balloons (ready for blowing up), fringed paper, a small calendar or diary, or bells. Or write resolutions on the package, paste on a scythe or Father Time or Baby New Year, etc.

WEDDINGS

Many of the gifts mentioned for other special occasions also, of course, make excellent choices for wedding presents. But, since a wedding means the sharing of two lives, the gift should be something lasting that both husband and wife can enjoy. A clock, a phonograph, records, a radio, television, pottery, glassware, mirror, picture, piece of furniture, tray, cocktail set, lamp with shade, blankets, sheets, scatter rug, teakwood vase stand, an antique, set of ash trays are a few suggestions in different price ranges. The list is practically endless, as anything for the home is ideal. (See store list on page 88 for more ideas.) Don't get anything that is likely to become a white elephant. These days, the combination of the beautiful and the practical should be everyone's aim. Don't get transient items like clothes or food. If you buy silver, don't get complicated pieces that are hard to clean and will hardly ever be used. Unless you know *just* what they want in this line, get individual spoons that can be used all the time for jelly, sugar, etc. Because of personal choice of pattern, the gift of silver tableware is perhaps best left to members of the family.

Wrapping suggestions. White or silver is the preferred color for wrapping. There are many printed and plain papers in pastel colors designed expressly for wedding gifts, and any of the white, silver, or pastel ribbons tied in an attractive bow will add that extra touch of perfection. You might use gauzy ribbon of white or pale blue, and thread a white flower through the bow. Trims might consist of paper bells, lilies of the valley, a white rose, a tiny bottle of perfume, a ring, a four-leaf clover, or any of the symbols associated with weddings. As this is perhaps the most cherished occasion in a lifetime, it is important that the gift be wrapped in especially good taste. A wise rule is to be as simple as possible, using good wrapping material. As the gifts are put on display, give a little thought and time to the decoration of the inside of a box.

Wedding packages with a color scheme of white and silver.

Use white or pale-colored tissue or excelsior or lacy doilies, and attach a ribbon or flower to the gift itself. You might line the box with velvet or silk if the gift is small. All these little details help to make the gift more beautiful and the occasion more memorable. An attractive effect, particularly suitable for weddings, is to wrap and trim a package in all-white, using different shades—off-white, cream, blue-white for papers and ribbons with a white corsage of artificial flowers in the bow. The fresh looking green stems of the flowers are the only other-than-white color needed for an enchanting package.

There are two other special occasions, besides the above (and the national holidays), when you may be called upon to give a present to a hostess, to children, or on a birthday if it falls near the date—these are Halloween and St. Patrick's Day.

HALLOWEEN

If a gift is in order on this day, the traditional colors for wrapping are pumpkin colors, orange and black. You could select any present that fits its purpose (birthday, children, hostess). Trims for children's packages might include cutout half moons, hayricks, witches, broomsticks, black cats, scarecrows, owls, masks, skeletons or anything scary. Some kinds of candy come in Halloween colors at this time of year.

ST. PATRICK'S DAY

If an occasion for a gift falls within a week of St. Patrick's Day, or, if there is a bridge prize, then you might take St. Patrick's Day as your theme, or the color green for your paper or trim. All kinds of ribbon come in green, green and white stripes, green and silver, green plaids, etc. You can use white, white and silver, silver metallic paper, or a different shade of green paper with your emerald ribbon and bow. Trims for the occasion are: shamrocks, four-leaf clovers, green carnations, green stove-pipe hats, clay pipes, green bells, etc. To be different, you might wrap a green ribbon around your package like a four-in-hand tie and decorate with some green knickknack.

THE FAMILY GIFT

Sometimes it is advisable to give one gift that the entire family can enjoy. This is especially true for someone who does not have much time to shop, who is unable to get to a shopping center, or who does not know the sizes, tastes, or needs of each member of the family.

Gifts of baked or canned foods, fresh-killed fowl or other meat, an assortment of vegetables, jellies, or a basket of fruit are appropriate. So, too, are candies, flowers, fireplace logs (unless you know their supply is plentiful), or other items for the home or yard.

Wrapping suggestions. Wrap foods in waxed paper (essential for fowl or meat), then, if you like, add foil or gift paper, and place each item in a larger container. A picnic basket, any large kitchen utensil, an attractive woven shopping bag (all of which can be used afterward), or a sturdy box may be used. A five-cent paper shopping bag may be decorated with seals, paper cutouts, or home or outdoor scenes. With a large bow tied on the handles, you will have a handsome package. Add bows, sprigs of greens, berries, fir cones, or whatever you have at hand for a pretty effect. Remember that containers for any gift can often be just as much a present as the contents. They provide that something extra that will always be appreciated.

THE MULTIPLE GIFT

When giving two or more items to the same person, wrap each one separately in a box of proper size and tie each with a bow. Then with the largest box on the bottom, arrange the others (if there are more than two) according to size and shape, turning the package so that

each bow comes on the outside edge and is not crushed by the next box. If necessary, fasten boxes in proper position with the Scotch tape hinge (see page 24). Tie all together with ribbon and add a perky bow at the top. An illustration of this appears above.

THE GROUP GIFT

This is usually more expensive than the personal gift because many people "chip in" to purchase it. It is a frequent occurrence at offices. Considerable thought should be given to its selection, not only because each donor should feel satisfied with the gift, but because the person who receives it will keep it in memory of those who made it possible.

There are many ways of collecting money for the group gift, but the fairest way is to pass a box with a slit in the taped-on lid, and let each person give whatever he can. With the money collected, choose a gift with a sense of fitness and appropriateness. If it is commemorating years of service with a company, it should be something distinctive like a good watch, perhaps, or a piece of jewelry, or a well made piece of luggage. If a wedding or Christmas is the occasion, several suggestions are given under separate heads in this chapter. If the gift is for a bon voyage or birthday, candy, flowers, or some small item may be given as a small token of affection. Both these occasions are also listed separately in this chapter.

Wrapping suggestions. Wrap the group gift elaborately, no matter what the contents, because it represents the sentiment of a number of people. Add a gift card signed by each member of the group; or if the gift paper is plain, have each individual autograph the wrapping itself. The latter is more unusual and effective.

71

READY REFERENCE CALENDAR OF SPECIAL DAYS OF THE YEAR FOR GIFTS OR GIFT THEMES

New Year's Day—January 1
Lincoln's Birthday—February 12
St. Valentine's Day—February 14
Washington's Birthday—February 22
St. Patrick's Day—March 17
April Fools' Day—April 1
Easter—The first Sunday after the first full moon after the first day
    of spring (better consult your calendar)
Mother's Day—The second Sunday in May
Memorial Day—May 30
Father's Day—The third Sunday in June
Independence Day—July 4
Halloween—October 31
All Saints' Day—November 1
Thanksgiving—The fourth Thursday in November
Christmas—December 25

Some of these days are universal gift-giving days. Others may provide a theme for birthday, shower, or week-end presents; for prizes; or, if you are in business, for good-will presents or window display package themes.

Suggestions for Making Your Package Individual and Amusing

So far throughout this book the emphasis has been placed on making a relatively simple and beautiful package. In this chapter there is no reason why we should not let ourselves go a step or two further into the realms of fantasy. On certain occasions and for certain people you can let your imagination run riot and your ingenuity need only be limited by the number of gifts to be wrapped. You can have all the fun you like.

Only a few ideas are presented here—just enough to stir your own thinking and to point out the enjoyment you can have as you plan gift packages for special friends—surprise packages that will amuse and cheer them up, make them think how much special thought you have given on their behalf.

For the Businessman. Wrap the package in the stock-market page of the newspaper. Tie with red grosgrain ribbon. Graph paper may also be used. If he is an architect or lumber merchant, wrap the gift

with a blueprint or wood-grained paper; tie with plastic ribbon, and decorate with nails, toy tools, a tiny bottle of oil (to help things run smoothly), and so on.

For the Nurse. Gift suggestions include a travel clock, a folding iron, a travel bag, dainty soap, sachets, lingerie cases, etc. Wrap box in white paper, tie with silver, and decorate with a red cross, an angel, a white cap (cut from paper or cardboard), a toy thermometer, or anything else that you think appropriate.

For the Artist. For your artist friend, use plain paper with a dull finish, or monk's cloth, and decorate with a reproduction of a famous painting you know he admires—a van Gogh, perhaps; a Picasso; or an old master—or, if in doubt, leave it *plain,* except for a ribbon corner wrap (see *Fig. 13*). You might tie on a paint brush that he can use, or a tube of color.

For the Beauty Expert. A package for the person in this line of business may be decorated with a purse mirror, a gay barrette, or colored cotton pads or tiny powder puffs pasted on to form a flower or corsage. The greeting may be written in red, resembling lipstick (or use lipstick itself). If the package is small, try covering it with a hair net to which you have tied tiny hair bows.

For the Sportsman. His package may contain golf or tennis equipment, a new gun, fishing tackle, moccasins, a wool scarf, or swimming trunks. Wrap the gift with forest green, ocean blue, or brown paper, or a length of fish net (use curtain mesh). Paste on colorful outdoor pictures of sports scenes. Tie it with fish line or heavy rope. Decorate with toy fish, trout flies stuck in a piece of cork which can be glued to the package, or with empty cartridges, bobbers, small sea shells, golf tees, a tennis ball, or anything else that you think he will like, or by which he will be amused.

For the Farmer. After his long hours at work and chores, the farmer will appreciate a gift designed to help him relax. A waterproof pillow for use on the grass, fishing tackle, a hammock, lawn bench, beer mug, a set of quoits or darts are gifts that may be wrapped in a novel manner. Use burlap and tie with fancy twine. If you think it will amuse him, decorate with corn silk, a small bunch of oats or rye, a small cow bell, toy tractor, or a horseshoe—or put on a few packets of flower seeds that he can plant in his garden.

For the Writer. The person who writes popular stories, articles, or advertising copy for a living might be amused if a small gift is wrapped in typewriter paper on which has been typed some appropriate text, quotation marks, dashes, or any typographical symbols. Tie with colored ribbon. Give a dream book or handwriting analysis book. Add a couple of pencils or a pen and pen wiper. Cut out ads of popular best sellers and paste on the package, or cut words from ads and form appropriate sentences or statements. If he is a highbrow, choose a plain subdued colored paper, decorate with real sealing wax, tie with plain colored ribbon, slant a quill pen through the knot of the bow—or, again, keep the package plain and simple unless you know him (or her) well enough to know his particular tastes.

For the Musician or Music Lover. Wrap package in a sheet of music, or use ruled music paper. Tie with colored ribbon, or wrap a package in plain white paper and decorate with five rows of narrow black ribbon run across the box to represent bars and add notes cut from black paper (see *Fig. 14*). If you are giving it to a professional or serious student, try at least to get the notes you paste on to make some musical sense. Copy a line from a melody you know he likes. If he is not too serious minded, trim with a toy musical instrument, baton, or phonograph record. If he *is* serious minded, play safe and keep the package simple but colorful.

For the Gardener. Whether man or woman, the person who enjoys making things grow will appreciate the significance of a pair of white canvas work gloves (especially if you flatter his or her vanity by stuffing the thumbs with cotton and wrap each thumb with green cellophane). Give a book on gardening or give a bag of humus, a garden stool or chair. If the gift is large, tape a slip cover bag of brown paper over it, tie with colored raffia or rope, and decorate with garden scenes cut from a magazine. On smaller gifts wrap in the ordinary way and decorate with pussy willows or artificial flowers. A gift of garden tools, bulbs, or light outdoor equipment may be boxed and wrapped with flowered paper. Glue colorful seed packages to top of the box or tie on a trowel or fork. (See photograph at top of page 76.)

For the Card Player. Decorate the gift box with an A-K-Q-J-10 sequence in miniature or regular-sized cards. Trim with score pad or pencils or cut diamonds, spades, clubs, or hearts from colored paper and paste on in fancy designs. You could also glue poker chips on top of the package. A novel wrapping would be thin green felt tied with red, violet, or yellow ribbon.

For the Sewer, Handicrafter, and Homemaker. There are many women whose hobbies have grown out of the activities of creating and maintaining a home.

For the woman whose hobby is some kind of handicraft, packages may be decorated with small balls of yarn, embroidery floss, safety pins, darning cotton, thimble, thread, buttons, or lace. A package may be wrapped with a yard of gingham, tied with bias-binding, rickrack, or ribbon, and decorated by pinning on a pattern envelope or picture of the item to be made.

Wrap material for a little girl's pinafore in or around a small package and trim with lace or embroidery edging. Run ribbon through the beading and tie a bow at one corner. Add a hair bow that will match.

Fabric is always a welcome gift to the lady who sews. Wrap each package with pages from an old pattern book, or paste cutouts of fashions on the box. Tie with a belt, bathrobe cord, or tape measure. Trim with a buckle, tassels, braid, fringe, or grosgrain ribbon.

Gifts for the homemaker are fun to decorate. From magazines you may cut out colorful photographs of attractive rooms or ornaments and paste on the top of the package. Or, if she loves to cook, wrap the gift in plain, dull finish paper, tie with gay plaid ribbon, and add cutouts of dainty food illustrations or herbs. If she is a decorator at heart, you may tie or trim the gift with curtain pulls or tiebacks. Paper napkins, cups, muffin-tin liners, lace-paper doilies, and the like may be used one way or another as decorations, or you can roll them inside a set of plastic place mats as a gift. Tie the roll at each end and wrap in cellophane.

For Grandparents. No one is more appreciative of the thoughtfulness you put into the selection and wrapping of a gift than those who

Food package (left), garden theme (center), for the traveler (right).

have lived through many birthdays and have decorated many gifts for others. This special age group is often neglected because of the attention demanded by the younger set. Young parents are often so engrossed in the selection of gifts for their children that they forget their own parents, or at best give them knee warmers or shoulder shawls. However, grandparents today rebel at age retirement from activities. There is no "lavendar and old lace" about them. They are alert, aware of everything that is going on, and want to be treated accordingly.

The longer a person lives, the more possessions he seems to accumulate, and it is sometimes a problem to select a gift for the one who "has everything." You may decide on a magazine subscription, a basket of fruit, a book-of-the-month, or a season's ticket to a series of concerts or plays. Potted plants, stationery with stamps, games, puzzles, handicraft sets, phonograph records (if they like music), money for a trip, a deck of cards, candy, new knitting patterns and wool, fruit, or food are just a few suggestions. In some cases a canary, goldfish, or kitten may be just the thing. You would know best.

Spend a little extra effort on wrapping the gift. Wrap lid and box separately so they can admire your artistry for a time. Make packages colorful and gay, with picture cutouts or with snapshots or reproductions of places where they have lived or visited. Or use plain paper with pretty ribbons or baskets that can be used again afterward.

For the Soldier, Sailor (or the person far from home). Don't try and make the package look like your idea of the port or country in which your friend resides. If he is a soldier or sailor, don't wrap the package in anything resembling khaki or navy blue. The person far from home likes to receive a package that reminds him of home or the people he or she loves. Wrap in gay colors with a fancy bow. Trim with a photograph of the family, home, or yourself. If he is your husband or beau, you might put a tiny touch of your favorite perfume on the ribbon to remind him especially of you. Trim with flowers or anything else that is pretty, heartwarming and you know will appeal.

When choosing a gift to be sent a long distance, don't send anything perishable, for nothing could be more disappointing than to open a package that contained food that had turned bad or a package of something that had broken. Check shipping regulations, duties, etc., at your local post office.

Gifts for Children

Most gifts for children fall into four classifications. They are designed to entertain, educate, stimulate the imagination, or fill a practical need. Whatever the gift may be, it should be chosen to fit at least one of these classifications, according to the child's personality, age and capacities.

An only child, for example, needs gifts that he can enjoy by himself, such as trains, musical instruments, meccano, a whittling set, bicycle, or dolls, to mention just a few. A pet is a fine gift to supply the companionship that an only child needs, but often lacks.

Miscellaneous wrappings. Note magazine "subscription gift" at top.

The too-quiet child should receive gifts that stimulate activity and association with other children. Games, athletic equipment of any type, roller skates, puppets, all are good. On the other hand, the overactive, high-strung, or noisy child will benefit from a painting set, crayons, books, construction sets, puzzles, scrapbook, and so on.

Where there are many children in the home, select gifts that may be shared and enjoyed by all—chemical sets, sewing outfits, building blocks, play money, games of all kinds, a toy farm, soldiers. If there are neighboring children, a gift that can be shared with others teaches the child unselfishness and helps increase his popularity. A baseball glove, ball, or bat; a set of quoits, darts, scouting equipment; a sled or wagon or doll carriage; and other items of this character are fine.

All children enjoy excursions into the land of make-believe. Cowboy outfits, Indian costumes, doctor or nurse kits, toy tea sets, kitchen outfits —all help to stimulate their imagination.

Of an educational nature, there are an increasing number of interesting items on the market—shell sets, astrology sets, weaving sets, books on nature and mechanics, encyclopedias for children, chemistry sets, butterfly sets, Audubon bird-carving sets, art appreciation books for young people, a microscope, stamp album—any of these are fun for the children while they learn something worth while.

For their parents' sake, however, think twice before giving horns, drums, whistles, or noise-making toys.

Gifts that fill a practical need (like clothes) are always welcomed by the parent, but are seldom exciting for the child. However, when such gifts are given, they should be packaged in a novel manner and trimmed with small, inexpensive gadgets—toy cars, airplanes, dolls, etc., to afford increased interest and pleasure for the child.

PACKAGING CHILDREN'S GIFTS

Children are not likely to be impressed by the artistry you use in making their packages pretty, but you can surprise and please them by using novel containers, gay papers, unusual tying materials, and exciting trimmings.

For example, a small pail with a lid or a tin lunch box is ideal for holding a ball or small toy and the child will have fun with it afterward. Tie a string of bells to the handle for a pleasant jingle. Or you might select a book bag, brief case, inexpensive overnight case, or small hat box that zips open as the container for a small child's gift. This container will keep a little tot who loves to carry toys about the house and yard occupied and happy for hours.

A small basket with a sturdy handle makes a good container for cookies or toys, while a loosely woven red mesh bag (the kind that holds oranges or onions) is an excellent container for building blocks, toy animals, and so on. Add a draw string at the top and tie it with a small bow. A plastic refrigerator bag will hold a small doll or other toy. If you have an old bird cage stored away in the attic or cellar, paint it bright red and yellow. Place toy animals inside, and children will play circus and farmer by the hour.

Paint any good sturdy wooden box. Add a hinged lid if desired and screw easy-rolling casters on the bottom at the four corners. Decorate sides and lid with appropriate color pictures cut from story books. The box will later turn into a pirate's chest, a Pandora box, a tool chest, or doll's bed, and it is also a fine place for storing toys at bedtime.

A strong corrugated box may be papered and holes may be cut for windows and doors to house your gift of doll furniture.

A tin cash box with its tray of small compartments is not only a novel container but a gift in itself which will be cherished by the boy who likes to collect things.

Children's boxes trimmed with Hershey's kisses and chewing gum.

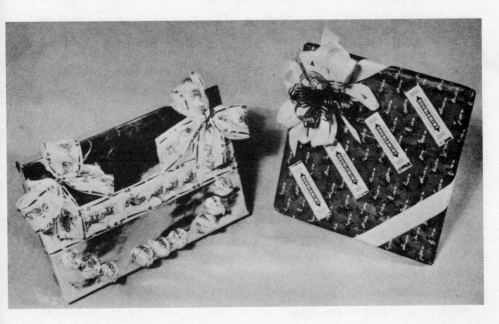

A wooden knife-and-fork box will hold gifts of knickknacks and takes up little space on a shelf in the playroom. It may also be hung on the wall where its compartments become little shelves for miniature china figures, dolls, toy animals, butterflies, framed stamps.

Wrap such gifts as a baseball glove, football, camera, or blue jeans in a red or blue bandana. Tie the four corners together and attach to a notched hobo stick.

If the gift is for a boy, tie with a belt or a dog collar or leash. Or use leather shoestrings which he can use later for his bow and arrow or on his football. Tie a package with twine, and place the unused portion of the ball of twine on top of the package to be used later in flying a kite. Even a piece of rope can serve for tying a boy's package. He'll use it later to haul his sled, or to practice knot-tying. To trim such packages, attach a bag of marbles for color, or a key ring or case, a money pouch, a small lock with key, a pencil sharpener. Gadgets such as this will serve to make any package more interesting to a boy.

Most girls, on the other hand, delight in dainty things. Use gift paper which comes in feminine colors and designs; tie with lovely ribbon of good quality, which in itself is a gift of many uses, and decorate the package with a group of ready-to-wear hair bows. Tie on tiny bottles of perfume, a cluster of flowers, a finger ring or a scarf ring, a fancy pin, gay pencils or crayons, soft toy or doll.

Package decorations suitable for either boys or girls include lollypops, Life Savers, Charms, gum drops, miniature books, soap animals, furniture, toy chinaware, little bells, marshmallows, jelly beans, puffed cereals, short macaroni, and popcorn. Any of these may be strung and placed on the gift in amusing arrangements. Paste new pennies on the package to form initials; spell out names with alphabet macaroni; or add color with kindergarten stars. Scenes cut from old gift cards, or animal or bird pictures from color ads or magazine articles, and characters from comic magazines may be pasted on sides or top of gift box or container.

Gifts That Are Difficult to Show

You've probably experienced that "let down" feeling when Aunt Matilda is proudly showing off her gifts but forgets to mention your gift of a year's subscription to her favorite magazine. It fills no space under the tree. Neither does the gift of cash, which although always welcome, is seldom displayed. Here is what you might do about this:

The Magazine Subscription. The magazine subscription can be dramatized by gift-wrapping an old or current issue of the magazine to be given. Roll the magazine and wrap with plain white paper. Cut headlines from feature articles such as "Ideas for Your Home," "Fashions for Spring," "Your Trip to Europe," "Gifts You Can Make," etc. Paste these printed headings on the white wrapper. Add the name of the magazine cut from the cover of another back issue, add a few colored stars or Christmas seals. Now roll the decorated package in cellophane, twist at ends, and tie with ribbon. (See photograph, page 77.)

Money and Gift Certificates. Gifts of money or checks or gift certificates may be framed. Buy an inexpensive picture of proper size at the dime store. Remove picture and replace it with the gift and a tiny card bearing your name. Add background of gold or silver paper or a square lace paper dolly. Replace cardboard backing. It is now ready to be boxed and gift-wrapped. Or make (or buy) a large colored envelope, paste a reproduction of an antique coin in the center, and tape a ribbon bow at one corner.

Another way of giving money is to make it into a corsage. Change old cash into shiny new coins at the bank. Wrap each coin in a 3- or 4-inch square of cellophane and twist tightly underneath. Wrap one end of a pipe cleaner (red, green, or white) tightly around the twisted cellophane to form a stem. Cut stems to desired length. Arrange coins in cluster and tie stems together. Push ends through a lace-paper doily. Add a ribbon bow and place in a box. Cut away a section of the box lid and paste a piece of cellophane in back of the opening so that the corsage can be seen through the top of the package. Tie ribbon around ends of box and add a bow at one corner. (An assortment of various colored postage stamps may be made up into a colorful corsage in the same manner. This makes an appropriate decoration for a gift box of stationery.)

Five or more new dollar bills will make a calla lily corsage (see *Fig.* 58). Fold each bill in half, crosswise, then twist it into a funnel shape and hold with Scotch tape. Next wrap yellow yarn or gold foil paper around one end of a pipe cleaner until it reaches the thickness of a pencil and extends about 1½ inches in length. Push unwrapped end down through funnel opening, allowing the yellow end to stick up at the top as does the spike of the lily. Group the bills to form a corsage and tie with yellow and green ribbon.

Ten or more bills folded in similar fashion and grouped to look like a

Fig. 58. Dollar bill corsage

little tree instead of corsage make a very showy wedding or anniversary gift.

Money earmarked for a vacation or a trip may be placed in a toy suitcase and tied with bows. Tie luggage tags on the suitcase. Cut place names from travel sections of magazines or newspapers and paste on colored paper cut into the shape of small banners. Stick these to the sides of the suitcase.

Tuition for a correspondence course, for music lessons, secretarial school, dramatics, the dance, college, or any educational purpose is sure to be a welcome gift. Package your money or check with a symbol of the course. Stick onto it an illustration or a toy piano, typewriter, comedy-tragedy mark, ballet slipper, college stickers, sewing box, appointment or address book. Any related symbol or novelty will dramatize the gift. Wrap the box and decorate with appropriate ribbon. Other trims might include a diploma, small dictionary (English, French, Spanish, Latin, Greek), horn-rimmed glasses, picture of an owl, etc.

A gift certificate which may be used to buy a hat, coat, china, silver, or anything else is often given instead of cash. This certificate may be packaged in a box along with a toy or an imitation of the article for which it is intended.

Many other ideas which reflect your own personality will probably come to you after reading this.

Plants. Practically everyone who owns a plot of ground would welcome a gift from a nursery. Strawberry plants, raspberry or rose bushes, bulbs, a flowering shrub or tree would make a pleasant surprise and assuredly would be a happy substitute for the umteenth tie or useless gadget. Since the planting of nursery stock is seasonal, order such gifts from the nursery to be shipped direct at the proper time for planting. However, a clue to your forthcoming gift may be presented at any special date. Cut pictures from a garden catalog or magazine and paste on the outside of the gift box. Inside place artificial flowers or fruit. Write a note or a humorous verse and indicate source and approximate date of real gift.

How to Decorate the Gift too Large to Wrap

The wrapping of the large or odd-shaped gift is a definite challenge to one's ingenuity and imagination. No boxes fit, and the paper is too small. To protect some large gifts, you might use large bags of the type that cover your clothes when they come back from the dry cleaners. Or you might use a cedar bag or even a garment bag to protect or conceal the tall gift such as a floor lamp or something in a large carton. Cellophane comes in sheets 40 by 48 inches and may be used on many large items. Plastic by the yard is not too expensive and is ideal for a large picture, mirror, card table, or small piece of furniture. So, too, is a plastic tablecloth which can later be used on the kitchen table. Oilcloth which comes as wide as 54 inches and in many pretty colors, will make any large gift you have chosen for your friend look attractive. It is surprising, too, what you can do with green or white mosquito netting for covering a big cushion, footstool, table lamp, sewing machine, and so on. A crinoline cover could even be made to fit the gift and it would cost very little. Wide wallpaper, too, may be used to wrap a very large box. Or, if you can spend the time, paste colored papers all over a corrugated box (most gifts from stores are wrapped in some such container) in patchwork quilt or decoupage fashion.

There are many gifts so pretty and glamorous in themselves that they need no wrapping. The addition of a big bow and a gift card is all that is necessary.

Another novel way of dramatizing a mail-order gift or the large gift (it may be a wheelbarrow, mowing machine, automobile, piano, tallboy, washing machine, refrigerator, sofa, etc.) that you cannot deliver in person is to give a miniature replica neatly packaged. You will find all sorts of toys including furniture and home equipment, in the dime store. Buy the one you need, package it prettily, and on the gift card simply state that the real thing will be delivered at a stated time.

How to Wrap Food and Candy

No gift could be more universal and acceptable in its appeal than food or candy. It is something everyone can enjoy and it is certainly a gift that almost everyone can give.

Wrap tempting looking foods in cellophane. For fruit cake, sausage, meats, etc., which come in grease-proof paper, use aluminum foil. Put cookies in boxes with cellophane lids or make window lids by cutting squares out of an ordinary box lid and covering the opening with cellophane. (This is a nice way to show off candy and nuts, too.) Paste a cookie or cake recipe on the top of the box, or make a little booklet of recipes and attach to the box with a piece of ribbon. Wrap jelly glasses in colored cellophane. Twist the top and let it flare out above the twist (see *Fig. 11*). The ends may be cut into a fringe or scalloped, if desired.

Foods may be packaged in tins, casseroles, bowls, jars, or other suitable utensils, which will also be welcomed as useful extra gifts. Give

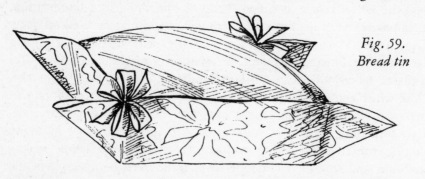

Fig. 59.
Bread tin

cookie cutter sets or cookie jars with your gift of cookies. Put eggs in a refrigerator egg box. An inexpensive pie tin or muffin tin or set of refrigerator bowls becomes a thoughtful gift if filled with food. Fill a bright new bread tin with home-baked bread, cake, or other food and cover with cellophane, then set the tin on gift-wrap paper and cover sides only, folding the corners outward as shown (*Fig. 59*). Fasten small bows to bobby pins, then clip bobby pins over folds at corners.

Any ordinary basket covered with crepe paper is a fine container for the gift of food. Fill with food which may or may not be individually wrapped. Tuck in bits of evergreen for color and cover top with cellophane. Tie bows on handles. Ruffles of crepe paper or ribbon or bands of paper fringe may be added to trim the basket. Some types of used flower baskets may be repainted with gold or silver paint and filled with packages of cookies or jars of jelly or fresh fruit.

How to Decorate Baskets

There are many different kinds of baskets—bushel, peach, grape, berry, market, egg, flower, bread, Easter; and they are made from almost as many different kinds of materials—straw, wood, reed, splint, cardboard, synthetic fiber, and others. (See *Fig. 60*.)

Most of us, whether we live in the country, suburbs, or city, save the baskets we receive, particularly if they are clean and in good condition for future use. Into these can be put gifts of fruit, vegetables, nuts, evergreens, pine cones for the fireplace, gourds, cookies, candies, jelly, ears of popping corn, eggs, and other farm products.

Baskets may be painted, stained, or varnished to make them look fresh and new. Old ones may be covered and lined with crepe paper. The bushel basket, so covered and filled with an assortment of farm produce or evergreen branches, is a most welcome sight to the city family. Or the basket may be lined with a plastic liner (on sale in department and chain stores) and given as a clothes basket. Put other gift parcels in it, tie bows on the handles, and no further wrapping is necessary.

The half bushel, hamper-type basket, commonly used for tomatoes or peaches, may be painted or decorated, lined with green or red oilcloth, and used as a wastebasket in an informal corner of the house.

The grape basket with its wire handle is easily converted into a doll's bassinet (*Fig. 60*). When painted or enameled, such baskets may also be made into flower containers by inserting a bread tin that will hold water. At Christmastime such a basket can be filled with bare branches, crisscrossed, into which evergreen may be pushed and held upright. Decorate a basket of flowers with the Greek bow (*Fig. 32*).

Small berry baskets may be painted or papered and filled with candy, popcorn balls, cookies, nuts, or flower bulbs. Wrap in cellophane and add a bow.

The market basket, wrapped in crepe paper which stretches around corners for a smooth fit, and decorated with bows, becomes the ideal container for the grocery and fruit gift.

Flower baskets are lovely in themselves and need but the addition of bows and some handle decoration—or you may, if you wish, paint them with gold or silver paint. Fill with flowers, winter bouquets, berries, or branches. Decorate with the basket bow (*Fig. 36*).

The flat or open-type basket, like that used for bread, and many shallow Easter baskets are ideal containers for gourds, Thanksgiving table centerpieces, cellophane-wrapped foods, polished apples, popcorn, home-baked foods. Decorate the handles only. If a cover is necessary, use a plastic one—the type made for toasters or electric mixers. The elastic edge will hold the cover snugly in place.

A brand new basket makes a fine gift. For instance, there is the sewing basket for a woman; a creel for the fisherman; an egg basket for the farm woman; a shopping basket for the suburbanite; and a picnic basket for the whole family. Sometimes too you can get cornucopia-shaped baskets which make lovely centerpieces for the table with fruit spilling out.

Stores and Departments
To Help You Think of a Gift

Everyone, at some time or other, is confronted with the problem of selecting a specific gift for a particular person or occasion. Throughout this book suggestions have been made to help you solve this as well as your wrapping problem.

Additional ideas for gifts will often come to mind if you read through a list of stores or departments carrying various kinds of merchandise. A partial list follows. Look it over before you go out shopping. It will set you thinking, and, by the time you reach the shopping center, you will have decided which stores or departments to explore thoroughly for your particular needs.

Fig. 60.
Decorated baskets

antiques	five-and-ten cent store	linens (blankets, quilts)
art gallery	florist	lingerie
artist's supplies	food (delicacies, fruit)	music (including radio,
baby's shop	furniture	phonograph, television)
bakery	games (bridge, canasta,	needlework
bathroom supplies	etc.)	notions
beverages	garden equipment &	novelties
bicycles	furniture	nursery supplies (plants,
blankets	gift shop	seeds, humus, etc.)
books (magazines,	gift-wrapping supplies	perfumes
subscriptions, cards,	glassware	personal stationery and
calendars)	gloves	napkins
brushes	haberdashery	pets
camping equipment	handbags (wallets)	photographic supplies
candy	hats	picnic equipment
chinaware (pottery)	hardware	pictures
cigar store	herb shop (spices)	pillow and cushion shop
closet supplies	home furnishings	religious supply store
clothing (adult and child)	home-furnishing	rugs, carpets
cosmetics	accessories	scarfs (handkerchiefs)
craft (hobby or toy shop)	jewelry (precious or	shoes (slippers)
cutlery	costume)	silverware
drapery, curtains	kitchen equipment	sporting goods
drugstore	knitting supplies	stationery
electrical appliances	lamps (and shades)	ties (scarfs, etc.)
fabrics	leather goods (including	tobacco and pipes
fashion accessories	luggage)	toys
fireplace equipment		umbrellas

How to Pack and Wrap for Mailing

Time and imagination have gone into making your gift packages novel and exciting, but when it comes to wrapping them for mailing, security and common sense count a great deal if all your effort is not to be wasted.

To protect your bows and fancy decorations, stuff the loops of each bow with tissue paper or soft cotton so that they won't get flattened. An empty box or quart berry basket inverted over the entire bow or decoration makes a fine protective covering.

For further protection, and to prevent the loss of small packages, place the gift box or boxes in a larger, stronger carton (save the good ones you get from stores). Cushion your packages at the bottom, sides, and top with plenty of excelsior so that each package is completely surrounded and will not rattle, or move around. Crushed or shredded newspaper or tissue paper may also be used for this purpose. For a single, fairly large package, corrugated paper may be used in place of an outside box, but the package must then be wrapped in extra-tough paper.

Wrap the outside box securely with heavy brown paper and strong twine, well tied. (Wrap in the same manner as shown in a gift wrapping in *Fig. 5b.*) Parcel post packages may be reinforced with heavy brown glued paper tape. But—and this is very important—if you seal your parcel in any way, you must attach a *STANDARD PRINTED* label to the package, which states that the parcel contains merchandise and may be opened for postal inspection. Such labels if *written or lettered by you will not be acceptable by the post office.* Official parcel post labels are available in chain and stationery stores. If ends are left free— that is, if you use only string and no tape—this label is not necessary.

No writing, except a signed gift card, is permissible inside a parcel post package. If you want to send a letter, send it separately or paste the envelope to the top of the box and put a stamp at first-class rate on the letter and separate stamps of correct amount for the weight of the package (at fourth-class rate) on the box itself.

The address should be written in ink or typewritten. Never use pencil. Write or print plainly. A return address should always appear on every package, no matter how near or far it may be going.

Use "This Side Up" and "Fragile" labels if goods call for special handling. Foods should be marked "Perishable" and it is advisable to send them special delivery. Do not attempt to send foods too long a distance. Those which will spoil within the time "reasonably required" for delivery may not be accepted.

Matches, liquors, pistols, and poisons are not acceptable for mailing under United States Postal regulations.

For a very small sum, packages may be insured against loss or damage for amounts up to $200.00. If you are sending packages abroad, you will have to attach a special card tag, available at the post office, stating contents of package, value of each item, your name and address, as well as name and address of addressee.

It is safer to consult your local postmaster for explicit instructions and for all mailing rules and regulations, as these are likely to change from time to time, especially on mailings abroad.

Pointers on Giving and Receiving Gifts

The manner in which a gift is given is perhaps more important than the gift itself or the way in which it is wrapped. Without graciousness, the loveliest gift suddenly turns into something meaningless and cold. No matter how artistic or ingenious you are in the selection and wrapping of your gifts, you can spoil the entire effect by your attitude.

The essence of giving may be expressed in one short sentence: "Think first of the other person's feelings." Giving is an emotional act; for a gift is a token of love, friendship, or esteem.

The appropriateness of a gift should be your first consideration—not its cost. The spending of a considerable sum of money on a gift for someone does not mean that he or she will be overwhelmed and delighted with your present. Quite the contrary. You may very possibly select something that does not fit into his way of life and even make him unhappy as a result of your thoughtlessness.

If possible, select the gift yourself—or *make* it—so that it bears the stamp of your personality. The man who gives his secretary money with instructions to "get something for me to give my wife" is cheating both himself and his wife. Even the busiest executive should find a few moments to concentrate on his wife's personal needs and tastes.

If money is the gift, you might earmark it for some particular purpose to show that you have given the matter of a gift some personal thought and, in fact, know what the person wants.

The woman who buys her husband a gift on his charge account cannot expect him to be overly pleased. Even if she has a joint charge account, it is better not to charge it on this for he will see what she has spent. Surely she could have anticipated the date and saved or earned an extra bit to make the gift a truly personal one. Giving in its best sense entails some sort of sacrifice.

If you are planning to give personal items, check with some member of the family, or a friend, on personal taste, color, choice, or size. This will lessen the need for exchanges. If an exchange is necessary, offer to do it yourself.

Regardless of cost or choice of the gift, it certainly deserves to be well wrapped. In no other way is your thoughtfulness made so evident and visible. Some people have the attitude that the gift is enough. They say: "It cost enough, why spend any more on the wrapping?" Others have the idea that some sort of wrapping is expected so they do the job perfunctorily and with little interest. Then there are those who enjoy giving, and show it by taking the time and effort required to make their packages express their feelings. They know, too, that the anticipation of opening a lovely box is part of the joy in receiving gifts.

When you receive a gift, show your appreciation at once. If the gift is delivered in person, open it immediately so that the giver can see how well you like it.

Before opening an attractively wrapped gift, make some flattering comment on the package itself. Open it with due respect and a proper amount of anticipation. Express your appreciation unstintingly for the gift. Should the gift prove disappointing, be sure to conceal your feelings, and never forget to say thank you. You never know how much time and thought has been given on your behalf.

If the gifts are opened in a group, as at Christmas, they should be opened one at a time so all can see and enjoy the fun. If children are present, let them open their gifts at the same time, or perhaps first.

When gifts are opened in the presence of many friends, as at showers, birthday parties, or weddings, give equal attention to each gift so that no one feels slighted. If duplicate gifts are received, any disappointment should be concealed, and nothing should be said by the recipient about exchanging one. If the person giving the gift offers to exchange it, accept graciously. It is well not to be too hasty in getting rid of the duplicate gift for often it happens that an extra may prove most useful.

Thank-you notes should be written promptly, especially for gifts received by mail. This frees the sender from concern as to the gift's safe arrival. If the gift has been lost, it can then be traced before too long a time has elapsed. Because of the many activities surrounding the Christmas season, or a wedding trip, a little longer time may be allowed in which to acknowledge gifts. However, thank-you letters should always be taken care of within a twelve-day period.

As soon as children are old enough, they should be taught to write their own thank-you notes, however brief, which the parent can include with a more detailed letter.

A Few Don'ts. Never apologize for what you give, no matter how simple or inexpensive your gift is.

Don't make the giving of gifts a mere commercial exchange of merchandise.

Don't splurge or overtax your charge account. There is nothing more disheartening than a stack of old unpaid bills. It's the *thought* that counts, not how much you spend on a gift.

Don't evaluate a gift in terms of money only.

Don't point out any difficulty you may have had in finding the gift, nor how much time you spent in making it.

Don't expect your gift to get all the praise. If it is appreciated, you will sense it. Besides, people who look only for praise are disappointed sooner or later.

Don't fail to remove price tags and sales slips from gifts.

Don't compare values among a group of gifts. No one cares which cost the most and it is in extremely bad taste—even among closest friends.

Don't take away another person's joy in giving by remarking that he should not have spent so much money. Just show how *very* much you appreciate his kindness.

Don't forget to let the person know what you did (or what you propose to do) with his gift of money.

Don't fail to make your thank-you note a personal one. *Don't buy a printed card* or, if you must, thank him or her personally too. Add some of your news, inquire after them, express a desire to see them, etc. Do not use hackneyed phrases.

Gift Wrapping as a Part-Time Business

Ideas are the initial investment of any business, and in the gift-wrapping business little else is required. A modest sum for the few necessary supplies; imagination; a talent or flair for color, proportion, and balance; and you are ready to launch a small business of your own. You will need ideas and more ideas, for it is possible to wrap thousands of packages, yet have no two alike. As you start with a few of the ideas presented in this book, others will come to mind, and you will become engrossed in the creation of endless varieties and combinations.

You may find that you have a natural talent for devising unusual packages. Friends will admire them; ask you to wrap special gifts for them; and before you know it, you will be in business. Or perhaps you feel that your community needs a gift-wrapping service; and so you set out, deliberately, to fill this need.

Whatever route you take, however, there are certain things to consider in setting up a gift-wrapping business. You will need a room or special place where all your supplies can be conveniently arranged and displayed in a businesslike manner. Place finished boxes as well as ribbons and papers on display so that customers can quickly choose the style and type of material they prefer. Have prices plainly marked on standard styles. If packages are individually designed, base your prices on size and cost of box, trimmings, and amount of time and skill involved. This will have to be worked out as you gain experience.

Have an adequate supply of boxes, papers, ribbons, and other items on hand to meet customers' requirements. Keep a good supply of all kinds of miniature knicknacks and gadgets, as well as berries, flowers, bells, and all types of small ornaments to help give your packages distinction and originality. Watch for special dates in the year that provide wrapping themes (see page 72). As your business grows and your purchases of supplies run to large quantities, you may find it profitable to buy from a jobber, or direct from a manufacturer.

How to Get Started. Send out attractive cards telling people about the service you are prepared to render. If possible, have a photograph taken of several of your best boxes and reproduce this in halftone or offset on your card—you must consult a local printer about this. Give your name and address and invite people to come and see what you have to offer. You can also insert an advertisement in your local paper.

Cooperate with your local gift shop either by offering to gift-wrap the customers' packages at a set fee to the shop, or by having the shop recommend your service to its customers. You may be very welcome—especially at Christmastime.

Get permission to post notices in YMCA's, clubs, small shops or stores that frequently have some sort of bulletin board.

Offer to give a demonstration of gift-wrapping before local women's clubs, church groups, etc. Also offer to wrap door and bazaar prizes for them free of charge.

Design small, attractive labels stating that the package was designed by you, and attach one to every box you make.

As an additional inducement to prospective customers, you may add a mailing service. For this, you will need to stock a few rolls of heavy wrapping paper, corrugated boxes, corrugated paper, gummed tape, string, thin rope, labels, mucilage, etc.

Commercial Gift Wrapping
Every day of the year is a gift day for someone.

Stores that sell merchandise suitable for gift-giving should be prepared to offer their customers a gift-wrapping service. The opportunity to have their purchases gift-wrapped creates in the customer an incentive to buy—making sales easier and more numerous. Furthermore, the store which sets out to create beautiful packages for its customers is doing a first-rate public relations job—resulting in increased prestige and excellent publicity. Another factor in favor of a gift-wrapping service—and one which is often overlooked—is that it brings the store's merchandise to the favorable attention of the one who receives the gift and inevitably builds up good will.

The Operation of a Gift-Wrap Department in a Store. Choose girls for this service who have some artistic ability and finger dexterity, and who enjoy creative work.

Provide adequate working and storage space, and see that paper, ribbons, twine, decorations, etc., are conveniently arranged so that not a motion or a moment is wasted. Ribbons and twine should be on rolls, paper should be on rolls or conveniently in piles at the wrapper's side. Decorations should also be within reach of the hand, but not in the way of the wrapper.

Use a distinctive paper of basic pattern or design, or use a pretty but unusual shade of plain paper that will be appropriate all year round and will come to be identified with the store. Use special seals on which the store slogan or name may be printed in small type. For denoting special occasions—Christmas, Easter, St. Patrick's Day, etc.—vary the tying ribbons as to color and kind.

Have several sample packages on display from which the customer may choose.

In some large stores, two gift-wrap services are provided. One is free and the other charges a nominal fee. It is possible to combine the two, especially at the inauguration of a gift-wrap service. Then, as the demand develops, you may find it more practical to set up two separate divisions.

In offering a free gift-wrap service, every effort must be made to economize on time, effort, and cost. In this connection it is well to know that a box wrapped as in *Fig. 5c* requires fewer motions and makes a neater package than one wrapped by the method shown in *Fig. 5b*, for instance.* Also keep in mind the fact that the diagonal, or corner wrap method of putting ribbon on a package (see *Fig. 13*) requires less ribbon, and with practice can be done more quickly, than any other.

In your efforts to economize, however, do not forget that the packages which leave your store become, in effect, your trade mark. Therefore, they should never look skimpy. For example, a large box requires

---

* *Providing the box is not too flat.*

a wider ribbon and a fuller bow than does a small one (the glamour bow [*Fig. 15*] is the one most generally used). The cost of the wrapping in relation to the value of the merchandise wrapped will in the long run, balance itself.

In any gift-wrap operation wastage becomes a factor to be considered. Odd pieces of paper left from wrapping one package may well be utilized on another small one. Similarly, odds and ends of ribbon may be combined into a bow of ends as shown in *Fig. 27*.

During the slow periods which occur throughout the day, have the girls make bows and other fancy decorations so that they will have a supply ready for instant use during the busy hours.

When a charge is made for the service, the packages may be made more elaborate by the addition of extra bows and the use of wider ribbon. However, the same principles of economy and efficiency should be applied to running the department.

Throughout this book, you will find suggestions for gift wrapping which may well be applied to a commercial gift-wrapping department. Also, most of the ideas discussed and illustrated can well be adapted in one form or another to make attractive window or inside store displays.

A final word as to cost allocation. Because of the importance of the gift-wrap department from the standpoint of publicity and public relations, the appropriation for this activity might well be made from the advertising budget rather than from customer-service funds.

College Colors (For Package Color Schemes)

Akron, Univ. of, Navy blue & old gold
Alabama, Univ. of, crimson & white
Amherst Coll., purple & white
Arkansas, Univ. of, red & white
Baltimore, Univ. of, maroon & white
Baylor Coll., green & gold
Boston Coll., maroon & gold
Boston Univ., scarlet & white
Bowdoin Coll., white
Brigham Young Univ., royal blue & white
Brooklyn Coll., maroon & gold
Brown Univ., brown
Bucknell Univ., orange & blue
Buffalo, Univ. of, royal blue & white
Butler Univ., royal blue & white

California, Univ. of, blue & gold
California, Univ. of (L. A.), dark blue & gold
California Inst. of Tech., orange & white
Carnegie Inst. of Tech., red, yellow, green & blue
Catholic Univ. of A., cardinal & black
Chicago, Univ. of, maroon
Cincinnati, Univ. of, red & black
Colgate Univ., maroon & white
Colorado, Univ. of, silver & gold
Columbia Univ., light blue & white
Cornell Univ., carnelian & white
Dartmouth Coll., oak green
DePaul Univ., royal blue & cardinal

Detroit, Univ. of, red & white
Drexel Inst., blue & gold
Duke Univ., blue & white
Duquesne Univ., red & blue
Emory Univ., royal blue & gold
Florida, Univ. of, orange & blue
Fordham Univ., maroon
Georgetown Univ., blue & gray
Geo. Washington Univ., buff & blue
Georgia, Univ. of, red & black
Gonzaga Univ., blue & white
Harvard Univ., crimson
Holy Cross, Coll. of the, purple
Howard Univ., Navy blue & white
Idaho, Univ. of, silver & gold
Illinois, Univ. of, orange & blue
Indiana Univ., cream & crimson
Iowa, Univ. of, old gold & black
Iowa State Coll. of Agri. & Mech.
   Arts, cardinal & gold
Kansas, Univ. of, crimson & blue
Kentucky, Univ. of, blue & white
Lafayette Coll., maroon & white
Lehigh Univ., seal brown & white
Louisville, Univ. of, cardinal & black
Maine, Univ. of, pale blue & white
Marquette Univ., blue & old gold
Maryland, Univ. of, black & old gold
Mass. Inst. of Tech., cardinal & gray
Miami Univ., red & white
Michigan, Univ. of, maize & blue
Minnesota, Univ. of, maroon & gold
Montana State Univ., copper, silver &
   gold
Nebraska, Univ. of, scarlet & cream
New Hampshire, Univ. of, blue &
   white
New Mexico, Univ. of, cherry & silver
New York, City Coll. of, lavender &
   black
New York Univ., violet
North Carolina, Univ. of, blue & white
North Dakota, Univ. of, green & pink
Notre Dame, Univ. of, blue & gold

Ohio State Univ., scarlet & gray
Ohio Univ., green & white
Oklahoma, Univ. of, red & white
Oregon, Univ. of, lemon & emerald
Pennsylvania, Univ. of, red & blue
Pennsylvania State Coll., blue & white
Pittsburgh, Univ. of, gold & blue
Pratt Inst., black & gold
Princeton Univ., orange & black
Richmond, Univ. of, scarlet & Navy
Rutgers Univ., scarlet
St. Louis Univ., royal blue & white
San Francisco, Univ. of, green & gold
South Carolina, Univ. of, garnet &
   black
So. California, Univ. of, cardinal &
   gold
Southern Methodist Univ., crimson &
   blue
Stanford Univ., cardinal
Syracuse Univ., orange
Temple Univ., cherry & white
Tennessee, Univ. of, orange & white
Toledo, Univ. of, blue & gold
Tufts Coll., blue & brown
Tulane Univ., olive & blue
Tuskegee Inst., old gold & crimson
U. S. Mil. Acad. (West Point), black,
   gold & gray
Utah, Univ. of, red & white
Vanderbilt Univ., old gold & black
Vermont, Univ. of, green & gold
Virginia, Univ. of, orange & blue
Washington, State Coll. of, crimson &
   gray
Washington, Univ. of, purple & gold
Washington Univ. (Mo.), red & green
Wayne Univ., green & gold
West Virginia Univ., old gold & blue
William & Mary, Coll. of, green, gold
   & silver
Wisconsin, Univ. of, cardinal
Xavier Univ., Navy blue & white
Yale Univ., national blue